Cooking with
Chef Silvio

To Carlo,
Di Cuore!
Any V. Rica

ee

excelsior editions

AN IMPRINT OF STATE UNIVERSITY OF NEW YORK PRESS

Cooking with Chef Silvio

Stories and Authentic Recipes from Campania

SILVIO SUPPA with ANTHONY V. RICCIO

Published by
STATE UNIVERSITY OF NEW YORK PRESS, ALBANY

© 2010 State University of New York

For information, contact State University of New York Press, Albany, NY
www.sunypress.edu

Production and book design, Laurie Searl
Marketing, Fran Keneston

Library of Congress Cataloging-in-Publication Data
Suppa, Silvio.
  Cooking with Chef Silvio : stories and authentic recipes from Campania /
Silvio Suppa and Anthony V. Riccio.
      p. cm.
  Includes bibliographical references and index.
  ISBN 978-1-4384-3363-9 (hardcover : alk. paper)
1. Cookery, Italian. 2. Cookery—Italy—Campania. 3. Suppa, Silvio.
4. Campania (Italy)—Social life and customs. I. Riccio, Anthony V.
II. Title.

TX723.S97 2010
641.5945'72—dc22   2010004838

10 9 8 7 6 5 4 3 2 1

To my mother, Maria Izzo Suppa, and my grandmother, Carmela Iannotta Izzo,
for inspiring me to learn l'arte della cucina, *the art of cooking.*

SILVIO SUPPA

To my mother, Lena Morrone Riccio, who tried to feed the whole world.

ANTHONY V. RICCIO

Contents

Gastronomy weaves durable strands through the colorful tapestries of all cultures. Invaders conquer, monuments crumble, generations pass away and traditions fade, yet food prevails as the lasting cultural relic that keeps family memory and ethnic identity alive. Though many Italian Americans have lost the Old World customs and provincial dialects once spoken by immigrant grandparents, Italian cooking preserves our heritage through "il linguaggio delle nostre ricette," the language of our recipes. Whenever families gather around festive tables to savor peasant dishes nonna used to cook, mouth-watering aromas wafting from the kitchen trigger appetites and fond memories of departed loved ones and reconnect us to a deeper cultural memory that reaches back millennia.

(above) Tin-lined copper cooking pot, Suppa family collection
(right) Farms in the hills of Benevento

Suppa family portrait, Sant' Agata de' Goti

Preface

On a warm summer evening in 2008, I received a call from Chef Silvio Suppa of Café Allegre in Madison, Connecticut. Silvio and his wife Vittoria were celebrating ten years of successful business, and they asked if I would give a series of lectures on Italian culture at their restaurant. Walking into the Café Allegre for the first time, I didn't know what to expect. Silvio and Vittoria greeted me warmly, and as we began talking our English quickly switched to Italian, then to the Neapolitan dialect of my parents and grandparents. One night after I had finished giving a talk, Silvio took me aside in the kitchen and, amidst the steady stream of scurrying waiters and hustle of assistant cooks, said, "You know Anthony, my dream has always been to have my own cookbook." I listened as he told me stories of learning the art of southern Italian cooking as a young boy from his grandmother on the family farm in Campania, a short distance from the farming villages of Alvignano and Calvisi that my peasant grandparents had left at the turn of the century. After trying some of Silvio's dishes that reminded me so much of my mother Lena's Old World Campanian cooking, I agreed to this book project.

During our many sessions recording his recipes, Silvio often stopped in midstream, switching from master chef to grand storyteller in English and Neapolitan dialect, recalling fascinating stories of an almost forgotten way of rural life in Contrada Sanguinito, his hometown in Campania. (A note on the Italian, we have used the Neapolitan dialect spellings and punctuation of Silvio's region throughout the book.) In March 2009, we went back to the *contrada* and nearby Sant' Agata de' Goti, where we met Silvio's family and many friends, who welcomed me into their homes with open arms.

I would like to thank the entire Suppa family in the Contrada Sanquinito for making me feel at home—Silvio's brothers Giuseppe and Angelo; nephews Clemente, Ilario, and Marinello; and especially Marta, Angela, Monica, and Antonietta Suppa, for cooking epic meals during our stay.

Silvio and I also wish to thank Mena Suppa for sharing her in-depth knowledge of Sant' Agata and taking us on great walking tours of the town. Many thanks to Claudio Giorgio Suppa, an enthusiastic supporter of our book project, who took time away from his busy law practice to drive us to Benevento and to Naples for our research. His father Mario, a quick-witted, energetic octogenarian, merrily drove us on trips through the mountains, pointing out castles and monasteries, telling us stories and legends about hillside towns we passed along the way. Our hope is to have his reflexes and sharpness should we make it to his age. Our visits to the homes of Silvio's aunts—Carmelina, Giuseppina, Giuannina, Ngiulinella, and Irma—in Sant' Agata were wonderful experiences, and they graciously donated old recipes learned from their mother, Carmela Izzo. We want to thank Alfonsina Razzano for recording and sharing her mother-in-law Giuannina's recipes for this book.

Walking the streets of Sant' Agata one day, I noticed Carlo Russo standing in front of his restaurant, the Taverna Saticula. Since he had the same last name as my grandmother, we struck up a friendly conversation and he invited us into his cozy taverna, its entry wall lined with linen-covered shelves displaying Carlo's jarred peppers and eggplants, homemade specialty dishes, fragrant cheeses, and fancy desserts on colorful terracotta plates. He invited us to supper that evening and gave us one of the finest samplings of original Sant' Agatese cuisine anyone could possibly experience. During the meal he brought out a fascinating manuscript he had written that traced the origins of his dishes to successive waves of contending invaders of Sant' Agata—Greeks, Romans, Lombards, Byzantines, Normans, and Spanish—through the centuries. When I explained the nature of my work, he graciously offered me a copy of his manuscript. His generosity and sharing of knowledge as a local historian of authentic Sant' Agatese cooking added a special dimension to this book. We also wish to thank Pia dePalma of the famous Strega factory in Benevento, who gave us a wonderful tour and encouraged us to include some strega recipes. I want to thank Giovanni DaRosa, *il fabbro,* the town blacksmith, for sharing his poetry and giving me two of his poems the morning we met on the Via Riello in Sant' Agata. Thanks also to Chiara Giorleo who provided a great tour of the Mastroberardino Winery and introduced us to Chef Francesco Spagnuolo, who donated recipes to this book. Many thanks to Dr. Leonard Chiarelli of the University of Utah for sharing his research on the Muslims of Sicily. Thanks to Simon Sameoil and Abdul Mannawi of the Yale University Near East Collection for their assistance, and to Salvatore Iannaccone of the Copy Catalogue Department and Graziano Krätli, International Program Support Librarian of Yale University for his help. Many thanks to Donna Clement of James Camera in New Haven, Connecticut, for her sincere commitment to this project and her technical wizardry to bring out the best in my photographs. A special thanks is in order for my friend and colleague at Yale University, Christopher Killheffer, for his excellent reviews of the manuscript and his love for all things Italian. And most important, Silvio and I wish to thank our families for their patience and support for this book project.

Anthony V. Riccio

Carlo Russo in front of his Taverna Saticula, Sant' Agata de' Goti

Claudio Giorgio Suppa, Carlo Russo, and Silvio Suppa at the Taverna Saticula, Sant' Agata de' Goti

I hope that every home chef will enjoy discovering the full flavor and goodness of my recipes. Like any cook book, there are variables and you will want to adjust herbs and spices to personal taste: what is salty to one person may not be to another; a teaspoon of hot pepper for *fra diavolo* may not be hot enough for some. The flavor of tomatoes varies by the soil of different countries. There is a story of famous pastry chefs who came to the United States from Naples with the exact ingredients to recreate their famous *sfogliatelle* pastry, but could not duplicate the same flavor or crispiness because of the different type of water and humidity.

Remember to adjust when following recipes with dough. When the temperature is dry, you may need to add more water; a humid day will call for more flour.

Salute, e buon appetito!!

Silvio Suppa

Vineyard in the mountains of Benevento

Introduction

La Bellezza di Sant' Agata de' Goti

Silvio Suppa was born and raised on the family farm in Contrada Sanquinito, part of the commune of Sant' Agata de' Goti in the Campania region of southern Italy. Nestled atop a semicircular plateau of volcanic *tufo,* Sant' Agata de' Goti overlooks the bountiful territory known as Sanniti, with ranges of olive groves shimmering silvery to dark green under the strong Italian sun. Among carefully tended vineyards conforming to the lay of the land are tracts of walnut, chestnut, apple, orange, peach, pear, fig, hazelnut, and lemon trees, and *lenze,* rectangular stretches of farmland for growing wheat for homemade bread and pasta, potatoes, tomatoes, garlic, lupini, rape, and oats. Across the valley Monte Castrone rises in the distance, terraced with long rows of *lenze* framed with grayish *murecena,* retaining walls constructed from excavated fieldstone, like large steps leading up the mountainside. A small chapel commemorating the passage of Saint Francis in the thirteenth century stands roofless and abandoned along a winding dusty road, a holy sentinel in ruins. Beyond the Isclero River, which cuts its way through the valley where farmers still tend the land and cultivate vineyards and groves of fruit trees, Mounts Taburno, Matese, and Longanorise rise majestically in the far distance, encircling the territory.

The streets of Sant' Agata are alive with townspeople meeting and gathering under arched porticos, in front of pastel-yellow and white stucco buildings, and under the shade of tree-lined piazzas. People walk with an easygoing pace, with time to stop and chat to a passing friend or relative. Undulating cobblestone streets hewn from *preta viva,* stone from local mountains, and cut into slabs of *vàsuli,* street pavement of various designs, lead to alleyways strung with open archways offering glimpses of walled *cortile,* courtyards with lemon and palm trees, water fountains, carved statuary on stone pedestals, and well-worn marble stairways leading up to entrances of private homes. On the street level, heavy wooden doors with iron latches open to reveal kitchens with women dressed in long white *'i mantesíni,* aprons, and *'i maccatur,* white scarves, busily cooking on traditional hearths and baking loaves of fresh bread from locally milled wheat in *'i forni,* the small wood-burning ovens built into the walls of their homes.

The sense of daily ritual, *il senso di quotidianitá,* of the typical Italian town is on display at midday when stores and businesses in Sant' Agata close their doors for the entire afternoon.

Friends and families retreat to their homes and gather for a leisurely, sumptuous, multicourse *pranzo,* where three and four generations enjoy eating together while engaging in spirited table conversation. Afternoon meals in this peaceful, charming southern town feel more like epic holiday celebrations of a bygone time. The Sant' Agatese revel in a cornucopia of fresh, locally grown produce for their *buona tavola,* the art of eating well, a culinary tradition that began with the ancient Greeks. Olive oil harvested from nearby groves, surely the gift of ambrosia from Greek gods, is flavorful and subtly sweet; it sparkles in golden-yellow streams when splashed over dishes or drizzled on bread. Wholesome homemade red and white wines without preservatives or additives, so *amabile,* agreeable to the palate, go down like springwater. Oral tradition recalls that farmers working in the fields of the *contrada*s around Sant' Agata always drank wine rather than water, abiding by the old aphorism often repeated at dinner tables, *"l'aqua infracita i bastimenti a mare"*—water rots the ships at sea. During my visit to Sant' Agata, I toured the Mustilli winery with its courtly owner, Leonardo Mustilli. After showing me how empty wine bottles passed through the mechanized production line, he brought me to a station where they were being sprayed and washed out with a light-yellow liquid that looked like white wine. When I asked Signore Mustilli about it, he explained that after hearing rumors of possible contaminants in local water, he voluntarily installed an extra bottle-cleansing station to remove any lurking impurities before the final wash. With a slight grin, he pointed to his wine cleaning station and said proudly, *"Vede, quello è il nostro vino bianco che usiamo per pulire le nostre bottiglie."* (See, that's our white wine that we use to wash out our bottles.)

Before the wristwatch, when a Sant' Agatese asked the time of day, the answer was given in terms of light, *"tre ore i iuórno,"* there are three hours of light left in the day. Sant' Agata's metronome, set when time was kept according the sun's position in the sky rather than by minutes of a second hand, still ticks at a pace for savoring life. Church cornerstones bearing ancient Latin inscriptions, plaques citing Roman emperors, fourteenth-century fresco cycles, and medieval water fountains constantly connect townspeople to their past, reminding visitors of the reverence the Sant' Agatese have for its old ways and time-held traditions.

One morning I rose just before dawn to photograph the town. Walking down the Via Riello, which runs along

Street in Sant' Agata de' Goti

the medieval wall of the city, I saw a thin elderly man walking toward me in the distance. Dressed in a collarless navy-blue workman's jacket with matching colored pants and cap, he exchanged polite "buon giornos" with me and struck up a friendly conversation. He told me stories about his life as the town's *fabbro,* blacksmith, known in the Sant' Agatese dialect as *'o ferraciuccio.* I was listening to Signore DeRosa with great interest, and just as the sun appeared over the distant mountains, tinting everything gold, he stopped his story in midsentence, paused, and said proudly, blue eyes sparkling, *"Sa, che mi chiamo DeRosa, Giovanni, ma sono un discendente d'una famiglia del secondo secolo, una famiglia Longobardo. Mio cognome era DaRoz, d'una familglia nobile."* (You know, my name is Giovanni DeRosa, but my real name was DaRoz because I descended from a family of Longobard nobles from the second century.)

Sunrise on the Via Riello

Campania countryside with vineyard

Chapter 1

Campanian Cuisine through the Ages

A famme fa asci 'o lupo ru bosco.
Hunger makes the wolf come out of his den.

Campanian cuisine began its evolution thousands of years ago around hearths of ancient Samnite tribes—Hirpini, Pentri, Caudini, and Caraceni—a rustic people of *massari*, peasant farmers, and *pecorari*, herdsmen and shepherds, who lived by a simple agrarian economy in small hamlets of *massarie*, with communal grazing lands rather than concentrated urban centers. The Sant' Agatese descended from the Caudini, who lived on the western perimeter of the Campanian plain in the Isclero valley and in the mountains around Mount Taburno and the Trebulani mountains. Samnite lifestyle was frugal and austere with few luxuries; they were a country folk in tune with their natural environment, deeply rooted in cultivating the soil and raising and tending herds of sheep, goats, and oxen. Rugged Samnite herdsmen lived in *case repentine*, small seasonal huts, driving flocks to the hills during summers and traveling long distances to the plains along ancient *tratturi*, trails across Samnium during winters.

The Samnites cultivated a variety of fruits, including *mele annurche*, apples, in higher regions, and grew *frumento*, oats, wheat, barley, and cereals, and *ortaggi*, vegetables and herbs, on the plains. Their principal foods were greens, legumes, wild game, various goat, cow, and sheep cheeses, and honey that they harvested from their own beehives. Unlike the more illustrious Roman and Greek civilizations, the Samnites left no ancient ruins to uncover, cities to unearth, or classical literature to preserve their legacy. Only a few bronze and stone tablets with inscriptions in their Oscan language survive, and most of our knowledge of them comes from the observations of Greek and Roman writers. But the modern-day towns of Cerreto Sannita and Gioia Sannitica still pay proud homage to the name bearing the ancestral roots of the people of Campania. During the great migration at the turn of the century, the Samnite name found its way to American shores when a baseball team of Italian Americans from Campania emblazoned

"Sannios" on their uniform shirts and won the New Haven city league championship in 1910.

The Samnites were contemporaries of the Etruscans and Greek colonizers who named southern Italy *Magna Grecia,* Greater Greece, in the seventh century B.C. The Greeks used a Campanian setting for their myth of Parthenope, a Siren who drowned herself in the bay of Naples because she could not seduce Odysseus. Roman writers described the Samnites as a family-based society whose principal form of government was the tribe rather than the state, a nation of fierce warriors who dared challenge the military might of Rome during three Samnite Wars, and fought with Hannibal, Phyrrus, and Marius in various wars until they were finally crushed in 82 B.C. Wealthy Romans who owned magnificent vacation homes in Campania called it *"Campania Felix,"* or Happy Countryside, because of its rich, tillable land, beautiful coastline, and friendly people. Paying homage to a land that produced crops year round, the Roman naturalist Pliny the Elder described Campania in the first century as *"Felix illa Campania,"* that fruitful Campania.

Centuries before Christian saints appeared in churches with miraculous powers to grant favors to the faithful, the Samnites worshipped in holy gardens with outdoor altars to honor their most venerated goddess Kerres, later Ceres, the divine patron of the harvest, cereals, and agriculture. Her holy intercession continues: Campanians are still blessed with fertile farmlands and 230 days of sunshine. They are a people who continue *l'arte della buona cucina,* the ancient art of preparing wholesome, nutritious, and flavorful food, maintaining a culture that never lost its connection to the soil. Farmers in the contradas around Sant' Agata still mark the changing seasons by winds with names: *'O Scirocco Che Porta Aqua,* the warm winds from Northern Africa in the fall that come before days of high wind, humidity, and rain; *'O Vento I Terra,* a wind close to the ground that ripples through seas of golden wheat fields; and *La Tramontana,* the winter wind cascading from the mountains that dries the skin and numbs the face. As winter wanes and the days of spring become longer, so does the stride of the chickens and their bigger farm brethren, the lambs: *Santa Catarina/Allonga nu pass 'i gallina* (Saint Catherine/The chicken's stride is longer) and *Sant' Aniello/Allonga nu pass 'i ainiello* (Saint Aniello/The lamb's stride is longer). When horizons blaze fiery red in the fields at dusk, the Sant' Agatese often recite to one another, *"Rosso di sera/Buon tempo si spera"* (Red sunset at evening/Hopes for good weather tomorrow).

The oldest known recipe from the *la cucina popolare* (the kitchen of the common people), so reflective of the rustic simplicity of ancient Samnite culinary tradition, is *pacche e fasul,* a hearty, peasant dish of macaroni and beans, flavored with thin slices of *'a cótena,* fresh pork skin, onions, tomatoes, and basil. Chef Silvio recalls his grandmother's step-by-step way of making *pacche e fasul* from scratch, with a few basic ingredients:

Old street in Cusano Mutri, Benevento

Pacche e Fasul
Homemade Macaroni and Beans

SERVES 4-6
PREPARATION TIME: 1 HOUR

When it was time to make *pacche e fasul*, my grandmother used to say, "*Mo facimmo' na pettola e maccarun' frisc*," which meant "It's time for us to roll out some fresh macaroni" and make *pacche e fasul*. She used to take out her *tavulill*, a large round wooden disk on which the pasta dough was mixed and kneaded. Then she placed it on the kitchen table, mixed flour and water, kneaded the dough by hand, added salt and pepper, and then rolled it out with a *lainatur*, a rolling pin, into a *pettola*. *Pettola* is a word to describe how the sheet of rolled out pasta looks like the rounded backside of a shirt or even a *pettola ru mantesín*, the hanging front part of a kitchen apron. Sometimes when my shirt was hanging out of my pants she'd say, "*Mett 'a pettola ra cammisa in du cazon*." (Tuck your shirt in your pants.) When someone was always distrustful, people used to say in a sarcastic way, "*Chill' si mett paura che 'o culo si roba 'a pettola*." (He's always afraid his butt is going to steal his shirt.) *Pacche* is an old dialect word that means something that is cut into pieces. "*Piglia sta' pacca e puorc e mettela ncoppa 'a tavola*" (Take this side of pork and put it on the table) or "*damme una pacca di mele*" (give me a piece of apple) was often heard in the kitchen. *Pacche* also describes how the macaroni for this recipe is cut in *pacche*, pieces.

After the pettola was rolled out and cut into long strips about three inches wide, she left them to partially dry for a few hours to a sort of leathery consistency. Then she took all the strips, stacked them up, and cut them across into half-inch-wide *pacche*. Then she laid them on a tray lined with linen cloth, ready to be cooked. She used to dry all the pasta the same way, including that for *pasta e fasul*, macaroni and beans, as well as other kinds of pasta like strangolaprievete, gnocchi, and orecchiette, little ear pasta. But I remember how, while she cooked these dishes, *'a nonna* used to sing in the kitchen, songs like "*Signorinella*" with verses like "*Signorinella dolce / della casa dirimpetta*" (Sweet young girl / who lives in the house across the street), "*O Sole Mio*," and "*Auciello Friddiglius*." Then, after I finished eating, for dessert, she used to say to me, "*Veni cà, a bella nonna, tu vuoi i fiche secche?*" (Come here, grandmother loves you, would you like some dried figs?)

In the years following World War II, pasta was difficult to find and she made her own, *maccheroni i casa*, homemade

'O tavulill e lainaturo

macaroni. The poor laborers had to go the *ammassa*, a distribution center run by the town with *a tessera*, an identity card, to get *maccheroni* according to how many children they had. Even *i signori*, the wealthy people of means, although they had money, had no food, and they'd come knocking on her door to buy chickens, eggs, sausage, and flour. Then they'd bring it home and give it to their cooks to make dinner with it.

The ingredients for this recipe are in two parts. The first is for *a pettola*, the rolled-out sheet of homemade macaroni. The second is for *'a salsa*, the sauce. You can also make this with *'a cótena*, using the same directions as *pasta e fasul* (page 20).

INGREDIENTS FOR A PETTOLA

8 cups sifted all-purpose flour (2 pounds)

1 teaspoon salt

Water

INGREDIENTS FOR A SALSA

⅓ cup extra virgin olive oil

4 garlic cloves, finely chopped

½ small onion, finely chopped

2 large celery stalks, finely chopped

1½ pounds ripe plum or other tomatoes, halved, squeezed to expel seeds, and coarsely chopped, or 24 ounces canned San Marzano tomatoes, undrained, and crushed by hand

Leaves of 1 bunch fresh basil

Salt and freshly ground black pepper

3 cups cooked white cannellini beans, or 30 ounces undrained canned

Peperoncino (crushed dried hot red pepper), optional

MAKING A PETTOLA

It's a good idea to make the *pettola* the day before or several hours before the meal. Place the *tavulill,* the wooden disk, on the table. If you don't have one, use a wooden board or marble slab. Place flour in the middle and make a well in the center. Add the teaspoon of salt, and then gradually pour water into the well while mixing in flour until all the flour is moistened and a rough dough has gathered into a ball. The dough should not be quite firm but malleable. If necessary, adjust by adding either more flour or more water. Scrape the work surface clean and sprinkle with enough flour to cover. Place the dough on the work surface, sprinkle with flour, and knead with your fist for about 5 minutes, or until the dough is smooth and elastic. Shape the dough into a ball or into 2 balls if easier to manage, and sprinkle flour on the bottom and top. Let rest for 1 hour. With a *lainatur,* a rolling pin, or a pasta pin, roll the dough from the center outward in all directions so that it forms a round sheet. Keep rolling and sprinkle the bottom and top frequently with flour so that it doesn't stick. Roll the dough between 1/8-inch and ^{1}/$_{16}$-inch in thickness. Let the pasta sheet rest for 2 hours. Then cut it into strips 3 inches wide, making sure the strips are well floured, top and bottom. Make 2 stacks of pasta strips and cut them across into half-inch-wide pieces. Separate the pieces with your fingers and sprinkle with more flour if needed to keep them dry and apart. Gently spread them in an even layer on a tray lined with a linen towel and let dry for at least 1 hour or up to several hours.

MAKING THE SAUCE

In a large pot, heat the oil over medium heat. Add the garlic, onion, and celery and cook for approximately 5 minutes, or until the ingredients turn golden. Add tomatoes, a dozen torn basil leaves, and some salt and pepper. Simmer, covered, for approximately 5 minutes. Take off the cover, stir in the cannellini beans, and cook for another 5 minutes, or until the tomatoes become soft. Turn off the heat and set aside.

Bring a large pot of salted water to a boil over high heat. Add the pasta to the water. Stir gently until the water comes back to a boil and the pasta comes to the surface. Drain the pasta, saving some of the water. Return the pasta to the pot, mix with the sauce, and add enough cooking water to just about cover the pasta. Bring to a simmer over medium heat, give it a nice stir, and adjust seasoning with salt, pepper, and peperoncino to your liking. If you like it brothy, serve immediately; if you like it thick, let it sit off heat for 10 to 15 minutes with the cover on. Serve garnished with more fresh basil.

Chef Silvio mixing flour and water, kneading the dough, rolling the dough, cutting into the "pacche," separating the "pacche"

Recipes in this cookbook reflect the cultural influences of foreign invaders and traders on Campanian cuisine. Greek colonizers of southern Italy brought grapevines to the fertile volcanic soil of Vesuvius, along with honey and sesame, in the seventh century B.C. Conquering Romans relied on Campania's rich farmlands to supply food for the Empire and introduced *laganae,* the antecedent of modern-day lasagna. The ancient Roman recipe called *salsa di pesce fermentata,* fermented fish sauce, is closely related to the salted anchovies used to flavor the modern-day classic dish *spaghetti aglio e olio,* spaghetti with oil and garlic. After the fall of Rome, Goths under the armies of Totila invaded and conquered Campania in the fourth century, followed by Longobard legions led by Zottone in the sixth century, who divided the territory into duchies.

Longobards in Sant' Agata de' Goti specialized in game dishes of all kinds, and succeeding Greek Byzantines from the Eastern Empire in the ninth century brought salads and other dishes like *insalata Greca: verdurina di Campania,* baby field greens, *dadini di pancetta rosolata,* small cubes of crispy sautéed bacon, and *crostini di pane arrostiti agliati con olio e aceto aromatico,* thinly sliced toasted bread rubbed with garlic, olive oil, and vinegar.

Arabs introduced many important crops to Italy, adding new accents and textures to Campanian cuisine. Muslim farmers in ninth-century Sicily applied advanced irrigation techniques to the island's arid soil, using water towers and reservoirs to grow lemon, orange, and fig trees, as well as artichokes, rice, spinach, bananas, sugarcane, cotton, and a hearty form of wheat

Pacche e fasul

known as *triticum durum,* which could be transported long distances without spoilage. Arab settlers in Sicily established the first macaroni factory, which made *itryah,* the form of vermicelli later known in Sicily as *tria.* This pasta was distributed to Calabria and Naples and probably to the maritime city-states of Amalfi and Genoa as well. In the eleventh century, Arab traders brought their prized eggplant to Naples. Arabic words incorporated into Italian document the considerable Middle Eastern influence on Campanian cuisine: *kharshufun* became *carciofo,* artichoke, *laymunum* became *limone,* lemon, *narangun* became *arancio,* orange, and *badhingianun* became *mulignana,* eggplant, in the Neapolitan dialect. Raisins used to garnish southern Italian dishes and *sharbet,* sherbet, made by pouring fruit flavorings on snow gathered from Mount Etna, also owe their heritage to the Arabs of Sicily.

Vermicelli alla Marinara
Vermicelli with Marinara Sauce

SERVES 4 TO 6
PREPARATION TIME: 30 MINUTES

⅓ cup extra virgin olive oil

5 cloves garlic, chopped

½ cup chopped fresh Italian parsley

2 pounds ripe plum tomatoes, halved, squeezed to expel seeds, and coarsely chopped, or 32 ounces canned San Marzano tomatoes, undrained, and crushed by hand

15 to 20 pitted Calamata olives, halved

2 tablespoons capers

Salt and freshly ground black pepper

1 pound vermicelli pasta, preferably imported from Italy

1 cup fresh basil leaves, ½ cup torn

In a medium-sized saucepan, heat oil over medium heat. Add garlic and parsley and sauté only for a few seconds. Add tomatoes and cook, stirring, for just a few minutes, or until the tomatoes soften but still retain their shape, without breaking down into a sauce. Add olives, capers, and salt and pepper to taste.

In a separate pot, cook the pasta *al dente* in boiling salted water following the directions on the package. Drain the pasta, return it to the pot, and add the tomato sauce. Add the torn basil and stir well. Serve immediately in a pasta bowl, garnished with the whole basil leaves.

Fettucine Alfredo

SERVES 4
PREPARATION TIME: 20 MINUTES

2 cups heavy cream

4 tablespoons butter

Salt and freshly ground black pepper to taste

2 egg yolks

2 pounds *fettucine all'uovo* (egg fettucine), fresh or 1 pound dried

1⅓ cups grated parmigiano cheese

¼ cup chopped fresh Italian parsley

In a large pan, bring the cream, butter, and a pinch each of salt and pepper to the simmer. Remove from heat, add the egg yolks, and immediately whisk them into the cream. Following instructions on the package, cook the pasta *al dente* in a pot of boiling salted water. Drain and add the pasta to the cream sauce. Add half of the cheese. Heat until bubbling, stir well, and serve immediately, sprinkled with the rest of the cheese and the parsley.

Rigatoni Casalinga
Home-Style Rigatoni

SERVES 4 TO 6
PREPARATION TIME: 25 MINUTES

⅓ cup extra virgin olive oil

1 pound Italian sausage, cut into 1-inch pieces

½ onion, thinly sliced

6 ounces fresh mushrooms, thickly sliced

½ cup dry white wine

2½ cups Chef Silvio's marinara sauce

1 cup fresh basil leaves, torn

Orecchiette con cime di rape e salsiccia

1 pound rigatoni pasta

1⅓ cups grated parmigiano cheese

Salt and freshly ground black pepper

Heat olive oil in a large frying pan over medium heat. Add sausage and cook, stirring frequently to prevent sticking, until sausage gets crispy. Add onions, and cook, stirring, until onions turn golden. Add mushrooms and dry white wine and cook for 2 or 3 minutes, or until the wine evaporates. Add marinara sauce and half of the basil and bring back to a simmer. Cook for approximately 10 minutes, making sure sausage is cooked through. Remove from the heat.

Cook the pasta *al dente* in a large pot of boiling slated water following instructions on the package. Drain pasta, reserving some of the cooking water. Return the pasta to the pot and add half of the sauce and half of the cheese, and stir well. If the pasta seems too dry, add some pasta water. Taste and add salt and pepper if needed.

Serve in pasta bowls, topping each with the remaining sauce and sprinkling with the rest of the cheese and basil.

Orecchiette con Cime di Rape e Salsiccia

Little Ear Pasta with Broccoli Rabe and Sausage

SERVES 4 TO 6
PREPARATION TIME: 35 MINUTES

1 pound broccoli rabe

1 pound Italian sausage, cut 1 inch across

½ cup extra virgin olive oil

6 cloves garlic, chopped

Peperoncino (crushed dried hot red pepper)

Salt

1 pound orecchiette pasta

1⅓ cup grated parmigiano cheese

Cook broccoli rabe in boiling salted water for 8 to 10 minutes until it's tender but not too soft. Drain and set aside.

In a large frying pan over medium heat, heat the oil, add sausage and cook until crispy. Add garlic and cook until golden. Stir in the broccoli rabe and crushed red pepper and salt to taste. Set aside.

In a separate pot, cook the pasta in a pot of boiling salted water following directions on the package for *al dente*. Drain, reserving some of the cooking water. Combine the pasta, broccoli rabe, and sausage in the pasta pot and add enough reserved pasta water to make it slightly soupy. Add half of the cheese and toss well. Serve in a pasta bowl, sprinkled with remaining cheese.

Linguine Puttanesca
Hooker-Style Linguine

SERVES 4 TO 6
PREPARATION TIME: 40 MINUTES

⅓ cup extra virgin olive oil

8 cloves garlic, chopped

6 filets canned anchovies, chopped

1 tablespoon capers

15 pitted Calamata olives

¼ cup dry white wine

25 ounces canned San Marzano tomatoes, undrained, and crushed by hand

1 cup fresh basil leaves, torn

Salt and freshly ground black pepper

1 pound linguine pasta

1⅓ cups grated pecorino romano cheese

½ cup chopped fresh Italian parsley

Heat olive oil in a large frying pan over medium heat. Add garlic and cook until blond in color. Add anchovies, capers, and olives and cook for approximately 2 minutes, stirring constantly. Add white wine and wait until it evaporates. Add tomatoes and half of the basil. Bring to a boil, then simmer for approximately 10 minutes. Taste for salt and pepper. Remove from the heat and set aside.

Cook pasta in a pot of boiling salted water following the directions on the package for *al dente*. Drain and save some cooking water. Add half of the sauce, half of the cheese, and half of the parsley to the pasta. Toss well and add some pasta water if needed to moisten. Serve in pasta bowls and top with the rest of the sauce, cheese, and parsley. Garnish with the rest of the basil.

Mulignana a Parmigiana
Eggplant Parmesan

SERVES 6 TO 8
PREPARATION TIME: ABOUT 1 HOUR

2 large eggplants (1½ to 2 pounds each)

2 cups all-purpose flour

6 eggs, beaten

About 4 cups vegetable oil for frying

4 cups Momma's Marinara Sauce (page 87) or Chef Silvio's Sunday Sauce (page 101), plus more for serving

2 ⅔ cups grated parmigiano cheese, plus more for serving

1 pound shredded mozzarella cheese

Slice each eggplant lengthwise about ¼-inch thick. Flour both sides, then dip the slices in beaten egg. Heat 1 inch of oil in a deep-fryer or a large, deep frying pan to 350 degrees. Working in batches, fry the slices on both sides until golden, approximately 1 minute on each side. As the slices are fried, set them on paper towels to drain.

Spoon a thin layer of sauce over the bottom of a 13 x 9 x 2-inch baking pan or other pan of similar dimensions, then add a layer of eggplant slices. Cover with a thin layer of sauce, then sprinkle with grated parmigiano cheese and top with a layer of mozzarella. Repeat until all ingredients are used, finishing with a top layer of sauce, parmigiano, and mozzarella. Try to divide the ingredients evenly among the layers. Bake at 375 degrees for 20 to 25 minutes, or until bubbling and nicely browned on top. Let sit for about 10 minutes. Cut into squares any size you like and serve with a spatula. Top each square with a little more sauce and sprinkle with a little parmigiano cheese. *E buon appetito!*

Suggestion: Have extra sauce on hand in case someone would like it.

Mulignana a parmigiana

Mulignana a Fungitielli
Eggplant Fungitielli

SERVES 4 TO 6 AS AN APPETIZER
PREPARATION TIME: 1½ HOURS

2 medium-sized eggplants (about 1 pound each), un-peeled, and cut into 1-inch cubes

Salt

½ cup extra virgin olive oil

8 cloves garlic, finely chopped

4 large ripe plum tomatoes, cut into ½-inch cubes

2 cups fresh basil leaves, torn

2 tablespoons capers

1 tablespoon dried chopped or fresh oregano

½ cup chopped fresh Italian parsley

Freshly ground black pepper

1 cup grated parmigiano cheese

Toss eggplant with 1 tablespoon salt in a colander and let drain for 1 hour. Firmly squeeze the eggplant by handfuls to press out bitter juice.

Heat oil in a large frying pan over medium heat. Add garlic and cook until gold in color. Add eggplant, stirring constantly, for about 5 minutes, or until eggplant cubes become tender but still retain their shape. Add tomatoes, 1¼ cups of basil, capers, oregano, half of the parsley, and salt and pepper to taste. Cook for approximately 5 minutes, or until the tomatoes are softened and the flavors are blended. Remove from heat, add half of the cheese, stir, and taste for salt. Serve hot or at room temperature on a large platter, sprinkled with the rest of the parsley and cheese, and garnished with the rest of the basil.

Optional: Toss the eggplant with a pound of penne, and you will have a beautiful Campanian pasta dish.

Mulignana a Scarpone
Eggplant Scarpone

SERVES 4
PREPARATION TIME: 2 HOURS

2 medium-sized eggplants (about 1 pound each)

Salt

⅔ cup extra virgin olive oil

4 large ripe plum tomatoes, finely diced

6 cloves garlic, finely chopped

½ cup finely chopped fresh basil

½ cup finely chopped fresh Italian parsley

2 tablespoons capers

1 teaspoon dried or chopped fresh oregano

1 cup grated parmigiano cheese

Freshly ground black pepper

Cut the eggplants in half lengthwise, leaving the stems attached. With a small knife, make crosscuts into the cut sides going halfway down to the skin, being careful not to cut into the sides so the eggplant halves remain intact. Line them up on a sheet pan, with the cut sides up. Give them a good sprinkle of salt and put them in the refrigerator for at least 1 hour.

In a bowl, combine half of the oil, the tomatoes, garlic, basil, half of the parsley, capers, oregano, and half of the cheese. Give it a good stir and season with salt and pepper to your liking. Set aside.

Squeeze each eggplant half with your hand to press out the bitter juice. Lay them out on a baking pan, cut side up. Spoon the tomato mixture over each eggplant, making sure it falls into the cuts. Don't be afraid to load them with the tomato mixture. Drizzle the rest of the oil over the top. (Some of the tomato mixture and oil will fall onto the pan. *Va bene*—that's good—because you need some oil on the pan.) Bake at 450 degrees for approximately 20 minutes, or until the tops are sizzling and crispy. Sprinkle with the rest of the cheese and parsley, and serve them family style or individually. If you serve them as an appetizer, cut them in two if you like.

Mulignana Scapece
Pickled Eggplant

SERVES 4 TO 6
PREPARATION TIME: 1 HOUR

2 medium-sized eggplants (about 1 pound each)

4 cloves garlic, chopped

Salt and freshly ground black pepper

2 teaspoons dried oregano

2 teaspoons peperoncino (crushed dried hot red pepper)

½ cup extra virgin olive oil

¼ cup red wine vinegar

This is a very old Campanian recipe. Trim off the stems and cut eggplant lengthwise in slices ½-inch thick. In a large pot of salted water, simmer the eggplant slices a few at a time for 4 to 5 minutes, or until cooked through but still firm. Lay each on paper towels to drain. In a glass bowl or Pyrex baking dish, arrange the eggplant in layers, sprinkling each with garlic, salt and

Stuffed eggplant

pepper, oregano, crushed pepper, oil, and vinegar. Cover with plastic wrap and refrigerate for at least 12 hours before serving. Make a large batch; it keeps for several days refrigerated.

Suggestion: This dish can be served as an appetizer or in a sandwich. For a milder version, leave out the crushed red pepper.

Carciofful 'Mbuttinat
Stuffed Artichokes

SERVES 6
PREPARATION TIME: 1½ HOURS

6 medium-sized artichokes

1 cup plain dry bread crumbs

1 tablespoon pecorino romano cheese

1 heaping tablespoon chopped fresh Italian parsley

1 tablespoon finely chopped garlic, plus 6 whole peeled garlic cloves

Salt and freshly ground black pepper

¾ cup extra virgin olive oil

1 lemon

½ cup dry white wine

About 4 cups chicken broth or lightly salted water, hot

Cut off the stems and about ¾ inch off the tops of the artichokes. Swish artichokes in cold water for 1 minute to release grit. Drain artichokes upside down on a towel. In a bowl combine bread crumbs, cheese, parsley, chopped garlic, and salt and pepper to taste, and mix well.

With your thumbs, open the leaves and force some of the bread-crumb stuffing in between and sprinkle the rest on top so most of the stuffing falls into the center. Make sure the stuffing is divided equally among all of the artichokes. Place the oil and garlic cloves in a pot just large enough to hold the artichokes upright; wedge the artichokes tightly together so they don't fall over. Place the pot over medium heat. Squeeze the lemon over the tops of the artichokes. Wait until the oil and garlic start sizzling and then add the white wine. Cover and cook for 2 minutes. Add enough preheated chicken broth or salted water to come an inch below the tops of the artichokes.

Cover and simmer for approximately 1 hour, or until the leaves pull out easily. Make sure there is still at least 1 inch of liquid in the pot to serve over the artichokes. If there is less, add broth or water. Serve individually in small deep bowls, pouring the juice and 1 garlic clove over each artichoke. Invert a bowl of the same size over each artichoke when serving. Use this bowl for consumed leaves.

Option for stuffed artichokes: Add 2 eggs and 2 slices of finely diced prosciutto to the stuffing, put into the center of the artichokes, then prepare and serve the same way. You now have Old World Artichokes Sant' Agatese.

Three main staples of Campanian cuisine—potatoes, tomatoes, and corn—came from across the Atlantic. After the Spanish discovery of America, the tomato plant arrived in Naples from Peru in 1570. San Marzano tomatoes, planted in the mineral-rich volcanic soil of Vesuvius and named after the town

Carciofful 'mbuttinat

in Campania, are considered the finest tasting in the world. They made Neapolitan pizza and its tomato sauce the most recognized dish among the world's cuisines. The milled cornmeal for "polenta" dishes, which became a major staple in the diets of central and northern Italy, came from American *granturco*, corn, around the same time.

Spaghetti Vesuviana

SERVES 4

PREPARATION TIME: 20 MINUTES

⅓ cup extra virgin olive oil

6 cloves garlic, finely chopped

2 bell peppers, possibly red and yellow, seeded and cut into strips

14 ounces canned Vesuvian cherry tomatoes, undrained, or, if not available, canned San Marzano tomatoes, undrained, and crushed by hand

1 cup fresh basil leaves, torn

15 to 20 pitted Calamata olives, halved

1 tablespoon capers

Pinch dried or chopped fresh oregano

Salt and freshly ground black pepper

1 pound spaghetti

1 ⅓ cups grated parmigiano cheese

Additional fresh basil or Italian parsley for garnish, optional

In a large frying pan heat the oil, add the garlic and cook until golden. Add the peppers and, stirring frequently, cook until slightly softened, approximately 5 minutes. Add tomatoes, basil, olives, capers, oregano, and salt and pepper to taste. Reduce heat to medium and cook for 10 to 15 minutes, or until the peppers and tomatoes are soft but still retain their shape. Give it a final taste for salt and pepper. Remove from the heat and set aside.

In a pot with salted water, cook spaghetti according to the directions on the package. Drain, reserving some of the cooking water. Add the sauce to the pasta along with half of the grated cheese and toss well. If too dry, adjust using the

Alleyway in Sant' Agata

Polenta con i funghi

pasta water to moisten. Serve in pasta bowls, sprinkled with the rest of the cheese and garnished with fresh basil or parsley if you wish.

Polenta Con i Funghi
Polenta with Mushrooms

SERVES 4 TO 6
PREPARATION TIME: 45 MINUTES

Polenta mix for 4 people

8 tablespoons butter

½ cup chopped fresh Italian parsley

Salt and freshly ground black pepper

¼ cup extra virgin olive oil

3 cloves garlic, finely chopped

1 pound of your favorite mushrooms, sliced

⅓ cup dry white wine

½ cup grated pecorino romano cheese, optional

Make polenta for 4 people following the directions on the package, adding half of the butter, half of the parsley, and salt and pepper to taste. Spread the polenta evenly in an oiled baking pan using a spatula. Set aside. In a medium-sized frying pan, heat the olive oil over medium heat. Add the garlic and cook until golden. Add the mushrooms and remaining butter and cook, stirring for 3 to 4 minutes or until the mushrooms soften. Add the white wine and salt and pepper to taste and cook for 2 or 3 minutes longer, or until the wine evaporates. Pour the mushrooms and all juice over the polenta and let rest for 5 to 10 minutes. Sprinkle with the rest of the parsley and grated cheese if you like. With a spatula, portion out and serve. Refrigerated leftovers can be served days later by baking at 375 degrees for approximately 20 minutes, or until sizzling.

Aunt Maria Morrone Capraro's kitchen, Sippiciano, 1973

Chapter 2
Miseria and Nobiltà
A Tale of Two Kitchens

A Madonna mann'u pane a chi nu ten i rient.
The Madonna sends bread to those who have no teeth.

Campanian cuisine and the social history of the region are intertwined like *menesta maritata*, married soup. By the late 1800s, millions of poor southerners found themselves hopelessly trapped in the *mezzadria*, a caste system based on unequal land distribution and disproportionate taxes imposed by the Piedmont government of the North. Farmers and laborers in the South lived a life of *miseria*, subsisting on meals of *'o tuozz' e pan e raurinio sicc' e 'na cipolla*, a piece of dry cornbread and an onion. Bread crumbs from stale bread sprinkled over macaroni dishes became the poor man's substitute for grated cheese. In the contradas around Sant'Agata, when someone asked the condition of a sick person, the answer was given in terms of bread, *"Annu mis' 'u pan' 'i ran,"* which meant the doctor had prescribed a diet of expensive wheat bread, easier on the stomach than the usual coarse, heavy bread, *'o pan' i cerza*, made with meal ground from the acorns of oak trees. Perpetual hunger and deprivation in the South whetted the Southerners' appetites for better lives in America and other lands, prompting the greatest exodus from any country in the history of immigration. In the South at the time of the *Risorgimento* (Unification), over 5 million, more than a third of the population of 14 million, left the country.

Campanian "alta cucina" haute cuisine also reflects the opulence of kings, nobles, and landowning aristocrats whose highly paid *monzu*, gourmet chefs and *fantesche*, maidservants, prepared rich, showy dishes for their well-to-do guests at lavish *banchetti* set in princely dining rooms. In stark contrast to the well-stocked, thoroughly equipped kitchens of the wealthy, Campanian cuisine also tells the undocumented story of the *cucina povera*, the kitchen of the poor, whose resourceful, imaginative women fed and nurtured large working families of *mezzadri*, tenant farmers, *massari*, owners of small farms, *giornalieri* and *braccianti agricoli*, farmhands and day laborers, and *pastori*, shepherds. For the lower classes of the South under the rapacious Spanish Bourbon occupation that ended in 1861, and during the *Risorgimento*'s exploitative aftermath lasting until the early 1900s, family survival often depended on a woman's inventiveness and ingenuity at creating meals with scarce resources. With time-honored cooking techniques passed from mother to daughter, women created delicious yet nutritious meals with simple recipes and skillful combinations of wholesome ingredients that enhanced the bold, natural flavors of earth-based food—the secret of their culinary genius and the soul of Campanian cooking—centuries before modern-day nutritionists and health officials shifted food pyramids toward the Mediterranean diet.

During the 1940s and 1950s, Sant' Agata and the surrounding contradas mirrored the rest of southern society. Privileged *signori* of the upper class—lawyers, doctors, and aristocrats—enjoyed spacious kitchens equipped with thermometers, whisks, and modern appliances like electric mixers and iceboxes. Maids were hired as family cooks and supplied with the best cuts of meat and high-quality copper pots and pans, *i tian' i ram*, which were thrown out when they became old. For farming women, handmade copper pots were prized utensils of the kitchen that lasted a lifetime. Because copper was potentially toxic if it came into contact with food (particularly acidic foods like tomatoes), pots were often given new life by traveling *stagniatielle*, tin smiths, who repaired worn handles and relined them with a layer of *stagno*, tin.

One of the cooking secrets of the peasant kitchen was the collection of *pignáte*, clay pots, and *tianelle di terracotta*, which absorbed heat from the fire without scorching, allowing legumes and vegetables to cook slowly, thereby bringing out their natural flavors. When daughters entered into marriage, mothers gave the *"dote,"* gifts of the bridal shower. Besides the traditional *curredo*, the marriage dowry of linens, sheets, and towels, daughters received the all-important collection of copper and clay pots and pans for their kitchens.

Food and diet reflected more than class distinction between rich and poor in southern Italian society. Italy's historic political, social, and economic tensions between industrialized North and rural South were sometimes expressed in culinary terms. Before pasta conquered northern Italian imaginations and appetites, northern Italians pointed to the South's high consumption of pasta, the main staple of the poor, referring to south-

I tian' i ram

Stagno

Tianelle di terracotta

I tian' i ram

erners as *mangiamaccheroni*, the macaroni eaters, a pejorative code word for uneducated, backward people. Southerners in turn referred to their northern countrymen as *polentoni*, the big polenta eaters.

Pasta dishes and cereals—the poor man's manna—had long been a simple local source of easily digested carbohydrates that quickly supplied the energy that farmers and laborers needed for long hours of manual work. In the 1970s and 1980s, American marathon runners discovered pasta's secret as muscle fuel, "pasta loading" before long-distance runs. Nutritionists and elite athletes discovered that the natural, unprocessed southern Italian diet—pastas mixed with beans, vegetables, and starches—provided a continual stream of energy during grueling sports competitions requiring stamina and endurance. Italian immigrants transported these simple dishes of the poor during the great migration to America at the turn of the twentieth century, where they later played a critical role in family survival as a major source of inexpensive nutrition during the Great Depression.

Pasta e Caulasciur
Pasta and Cauliflower Soup

SERVES 6

PREPARATION TIME: 45 MINUTES

⅓ cup extra virgin olive oil

1 cup onions, finely chopped

4 cloves garlic, finely chopped

1 large celery stalk, finely chopped

½ cup dry white wine

1 medium-sized cauliflower, cleaned and cut into small florets

2 cups ripe plum tomatoes, cut into ½-inch dice

½ cup fresh basil leaves, torn

Salt and freshly ground black pepper

About 4 cups chicken broth or water

1 pound ditalini pasta (or your favorite small pasta)

½ cup chopped fresh Italian parsley

1 cup grated parmigiano cheese

Heat oil in a large pot over high heat, then add onion, garlic, and celery. Cook, stirring frequently, until the vegetables turn golden. Add white wine and let reduce for 1 minute. Stir in cauliflower, tomatoes, and basil, then season with salt and pepper and cook for 2 minutes. Add enough chicken broth or water to cover contents. Lower heat and let simmer for approximately 10 minutes, or until cauliflower is cooked *al dente*. Remove from the heat and set aside.

Cook the pasta *al dente* in a pot of boiling salted water following instructions on the package. Drain, reserving some of the cooking water. Add the pasta to the cauliflower, return to high heat, and add, if necessary, enough reserved cooking water to cover the cauliflower. Bring all back to a boil, stir, and taste for salt and pepper. Adjust consistency to your liking with additional pasta water. Serve in deep bowls, sprinkled with chopped parsley and parmigiano cheese. Add peperoncino (crushed dried hot red pepper) for a spicier version. For a vegetarian version, make the soup with water or vegetable broth.

Pasta e Patan
Pasta and Potatoes

SERVES 6

PREPARATION TIME: 30 TO 45 MINUTES

⅓ cup extra virgin olive oil

1 medium-sized onion, finely chopped

4 cloves garlic, finely chopped

2 pounds potatoes, cut into ½-inch cubes

2 cups chopped ripe plum tomatoes

½ cup fresh basil leaves, torn

Salt and freshly ground black pepper

About 4 cups chicken broth or water

1 pound lumachelle ("little snails") pasta (or your favorite small pasta)

½ cup chopped fresh Italian parsley

1 cup grated parmigiano cheese

Place a large pot over high heat. Add olive oil, onion, and garlic and cook, stirring frequently until onions and garlic are golden. Add potatoes, tomatoes, basil, and salt and pepper to taste and cook, stirring, until sizzling. Add enough chicken broth or water to cover the contents. Bring to a boil, then turn the heat down to medium and cook for approximately 10 minutes, or until potatoes are tender but still keep their shape. Remove from the heat and set aside.

Cook the pasta *al dente* in a pot of boiling salted water following instructions on the package. Drain the pasta, reserving

Pasta e piselli

some of the cooking water. Add the pasta to the potato mixture, set over high heat, and, if necessary, enough reserved pasta water to cover the contents. Bring all back to a boil, stir, and taste for salt and pepper. Adjust consistency to your liking with additional pasta water. Serve in deep bowls, sprinkled with chopped parsley, and parmigiano cheese.

Optional: Add peperoncino (crushed dried hot red pepper) for a spicier version. For a vegetarian version, make the soup with water or vegetable broth.

Pasta e Piselli
Pasta and Peas

SERVES 6
PREPARATION TIME: 30 TO 45 MINUTES

⅓ cup extra virgin olive oil

1 medium-sized onion, chopped

3 cloves garlic, chopped

3 ounces end or scrap piece prosciutto, cut into julienne strips

1 pound frozen or shelled green peas

2 cups chopped ripe tomatoes, preferably plum

1 cup fresh basil leaves, torn

Salt and freshly ground black pepper

About 2 cups chicken broth or water

1 pound ditalini pasta (or your favorite small pasta)

½ cup chopped fresh Italian parsley

½ cup grated parmigiano cheese

In a large pot over high heat, combine extra virgin olive oil, onion, garlic, and prosciutto. Stirring occasionally, cook until the onion and garlic are golden. Add the peas, tomatoes, half of the basil, salt, pepper, and just enough chicken broth to cover the peas. Bring to a boil, turn down the heat to medium and simmer for 8 to 10 minutes until peas are cooked. Remove from the heat and set aside.

Cook the pasta *al dente* in a pot of boiling salted water, following instructions on the package. Drain the pasta, reserving some of the cooking water. Add the pasta to the pea mixture, set over high heat, and, if necessary, add enough pasta water to cover the peas. Bring all back to a boil, stir, and taste for salt and pepper. Adjust consistency according to your liking with additional pasta water. Serve in deep bowls, sprinkled with chopped parsley and parmigiano cheese. Garnish with the rest of the basil.

Optional: Add peperoncino (crushed dried hot red pepper) for a spicier version. For vegetarian version, leave out the prosciutto and make the dish with water.

Pasta e Ceci
Pasta and Chickpeas

SERVES 6 TO 8

PREPARATION TIME: 25 TO 30 MINUTES

⅓ cup extra virgin olive oil

8 to 10 cloves garlic, chopped

4 cups cooked chickpeas, or 32 ounces undrained canned

½ cup chopped fresh Italian parsley

About 4 cups chicken broth or water

Salt and freshly ground black pepper

1 pound elbow pasta (or other small pasta)

1 cup grated parmigiano cheese

In a large pot over high heat, combine the oil and garlic and cook, stirring, until the garlic is golden. Add chickpeas, half of the parsley, and enough chicken broth or water to cover the chickpeas. Add salt and pepper to taste. Bring contents to a boil. Remove from the heat and set aside.

Cook the pasta *al dente* in a pot of boiling salted water following instructions on the package. Drain pasta, reserving some of the cooking water. Add the pasta to the chickpea mixture, return to high heat and, if necessary, add enough pasta water to cover the chickpeas. Bring all back to a boil, stir, and taste for salt and pepper. Add more pasta water if needed to moisten. Serve in deep bowls, sprinkled with remaining chopped parsley and parmigiano cheese.

Optional: Add peperoncino for a spicier version. For a vegetarian version, make the dish with water.

Pasta e ceci

Pasta e Fasul
Pasta and Beans

SERVES 6

PREPARATION TIME: 30 TO 40 MINUTES

⅓ cup extra virgin olive oil

8 slices smoked bacon, finely diced

½ onion, finely chopped

1 celery stalk, finely chopped

1½ cups marinara sauce (page 87), Chef Silvio's
  Capricciosa Sauce, or your favorite marinara sauce

3 cups cooked white cannellini beans, or 30 ounces
  undrained canned

1 pound tubettini or ditalini pasta (or your favorite
  small pasta)

1 cup fresh basil leaves, torn

½ cup chopped fresh Italian parsley

Salt and freshly ground black pepper

Peperoncino (crushed dried hot red pepper),
  optional

1 cup grated parmigiano cheese

Heat oil in a large pot over medium heat. Add bacon and cook, stirring frequently until crispy. Add onion and celery and continue to cook, stirring, until the onions are golden. Add sauce and cannellini beans, bring back to a boil. Remove from the heat and set aside.

In a separate pot, cook the pasta *al dente* in boiling salted water, following the directions on the package. Drain pasta, reserving some of the cooking water. Add the pasta to the beans, then add enough pasta water to cover the contents. Add half of the basil, half of the parsley, and salt, black pepper to taste, and, if you like, peperoncino (crushed red pepper). Stir well. Bring to a boil over medium heat and then reduce the heat and simmer for about 3 minutes. Remove from the heat and add cheese. Check for seasoning and adjust the consistency with additional pasta water, making it soupy or thick, to your liking. Serve in deep bowls, sprinkled with the rest of the parsley and basil.

Pasta e Fasul ca' Cótena
Macaroni and Beans with Pork Skin

SERVES 6

PREPARATION TIME: 1 HOUR AND 20 MINUTES

My grandmother used to put her dried cannellini beans in water overnight to soak. The next morning she drained them and put them into a clay *pignáta* with fresh water and *'a cótena*, pig skin. She put the *pignáta* in the fireplace next to the fire and let the beans cook for an hour, or until they became tender to the bite. Today, a *pignáta* like my grandmother's is nearly impossible to find, so use a regular pot on the stove. This recipe is almost the same as *pasta e fasul*, except that you add *cótena* to the cannellini beans. When both are cooked, take the *cótena* out and cut it into julienne strips. Then add the beans and the *cótena* to the sauce. Serve in deep bowls and garnish with parsley or basil.

⅓ cup extra virgin olive oil

4 to 5 ounces *guanciale*, cured pig cheek, or 8 slices of
  smoked bacon, finely diced

½ onion, finely chopped

1 celery stalk, finely chopped

1½ cups marinara sauce

3 cups cooked white cannellini beans, or 30 ounces
  undrained canned

6 to 8 ounces fresh *cótena*, pig skin, boiled for 1 hour or
  until soft, and cut into julienne strips

1 pound tubettini or ditalini pasta (or other small pasta)

12 fresh basil leaves, torn or coarsely chopped

½ cup chopped fresh Italian parsley

Salt and freshly ground black pepper

Peperoncino (crushed dried hot red pepper), optional

1 cup grated parmigiano cheese

Heat oil in a large pot over medium heat. Add the *guanciale* or bacon and cook, stirring frequently until crispy. Add onion and celery and continue to cook, stirring, until the vegetables are golden. Add sauce, cannellini beans, and *'a cótena*, stir, and bring back to a boil. Remove from the heat and set aside.

In another pot, cook pasta *al dente* in boiling salted water, following the directions on the package. Drain the pasta, reserving some of the cooking water. Add the pasta to the bean mixture along with enough pasta water to cover the contents. Place over medium heat and add the basil, half of the parsley, and salt, black pepper, and crushed red pepper (if you like), to taste. Stir well. Bring back to a boil, then reduce heat and simmer for about 3 minutes. Remove from heat and add cheese. Check for seasoning. If you like it soupy, add more pasta water and serve immediately; if you like it thicker, let it sit for 5 minutes. Sprinkle with remaining parsley.

Pasta e Cucozza
Pasta with Pumpkin

SERVES 6 TO 8

PREPARATION TIME: 30 MINUTES

My grandfather Angelo used to plant pumpkins for cooking and to feed the animals—pigs, cows, and horses. When these pumpkins, *cucozze*, had fully matured, we made *pasta e cucozza*, pasta with pumpkin, and pumpkin soup. We also made *torte di zucche*, pumpkin pies. My grandfather saved the seeds and planted some the following year. The rest of the seeds were dried in the sun and eaten with wine around the fireplace. We used pumpkins to feed the rabbits, and chickens too.

½ cup extra virgin olive oil

6 cloves garlic, finely chopped

4 cups cooking pumpkin, such as Small Sugar, or butternut squash, seeded, peeled, and cubed

1 cup dry white wine

2 cups cooked white cannellini beans or 20 ounces undrained canned

1 cup chopped fresh Italian parsley

1 teaspoon peperoncino (crushed dried red pepper)

Salt and freshly ground black pepper to taste

About 4 cups chicken broth or water

1 pound spaghetti, broken into 1½-inch pieces

2 cups grated parmigiano cheese

Heat oil in a large pot over high heat. Add garlic and cook, stirring, until garlic is blond in color. Add pumpkin and white

November olive harvest

wine and cook for 5 minutes with the cover on. Give it a good stir and continue to cook, covered, until pumpkin starts to break apart. Add cannellini beans, half of the parsley, hot red pepper, and salt and black pepper to taste. Add enough liquid to nearly cover the contents. Bring all back to a boil, then remove from the heat and set aside.

In a separate pot, cook pasta *al dente* in a pot of salted boiling water according to the directions on the package. Drain and add to pumpkin, reserving some of the cooking water. Add 1½ cups of the parmigiano cheese, taste for seasoning, and thin, if necessary, with pasta water. Serve in deep bowls, sprinkled with the remaining cheese and parsley.

Zuppa di Zucca
Pumpkin Soup

SERVES 6 TO 8
PREPARATION TIME: 45 MINUTES

¼ cup extra virgin olive oil

4 large cloves garlic, minced

2 tablespoons butter

2 pounds cooking pumpkin, such as Small Sugar, or butternut squash, seeded, peeled, and cubed

½ teaspoon minced hot cherry pepper

1 cup dry white wine

Salt and freshly ground black pepper

6 cups chicken broth

One 15-ounce can white cannellini beans, well drained

1 cup grated parmigiano cheese

½ cup chopped fresh Italian parsley

8 ounces ditalini pasta, cooked

Heat oil in a large pot over high heat. Add the garlic and sauté until golden. Add butter, pumpkin, and cherry pepper. Sauté until pumpkin begins to soften, about 5 minutes. Add white wine and salt and pepper to taste. Bring wine to a boil and cook until almost completely evaporated. Add broth and bring to a boil. Reduce heat and simmer until pumpkin is soft, 15 to 20 minutes. Cubes should start to break apart but still be a bit chunky. Add beans, half of the grated cheese, and half of the parsley and cook until it comes back to a boil. Add cooked pasta to individual bowls, then add soup. Sprinkle with the rest of the parmigiano cheese and parsley and serve.

Minestrone Napulitano
Neapolitan Minestrone Soup

SERVES 8 TO 10
PREPARATION TIME: 1 HOUR

⅓ cup extra virgin olive oil

1 cup onions cut into ½-inch dice

1 cup celery cut into ½-inch dice

1 cup peeled carrots cut into ½-inch dice

1 cup zucchini cut into ½-inch dice

1 cup potatoes cut into ½-inch dice

1 cup ripe tomatoes cut into ½-inch dice

12 fresh basil leaves, torn

About 6 cups chicken broth or water

½ cup cooked or well-drained canned white cannellini beans

½ cup cooked or well-drained canned red cannellini beans

½ cup cooked or well-drained canned chickpeas

½ cup frozen or shelled fresh green peas

Salt and freshly ground black pepper

Grated parmigiano cheese and chopped fresh Italian parsley for serving

Heat oil in a large pot over medium heat. Add onion and cook, stirring, until translucent. Add celery, carrots, zucchini, potatoes, tomatoes, and basil. Give contents a good stir. Add enough chicken broth or water to cover vegetables by about 2 inches. Simmer until vegetables are *al dente*, always keeping vegetables well covered with liquid. Add beans, chickpeas and green peas. Bring back to a simmer and season with salt and pepper to your liking. Serve sprinkled with grated cheese and parsley to your liking.

Kitchens of the wealthy and poor intersected throughout Italian culinary history. Upper-class families in ancient Rome employed chefs and their assistants, who drew their inspiration from the simple yet tasty food of *la cucina della povera gente*, the kitchen of the poor people. They learned local country ways of cooking from shepherds and farmers—tasty local fish, *caciottelle* cheese from Irpinia, goats and lamb from Abruzzo and the Ciociaria area around Rome—to create Roman cuisine. At the conclusion of royal banquets at the Angevin palace in thirteenth-century Naples, throngs of poor Neapolitan women ran to the call of *"les entrailles"* from French servants of the king, who handed out leftover entrails of freshly butchered meats. Via the French word *entrailles*, these women became known as *zantraglie*, the poor dressed in rags. When these creative women returned to their humble kitchens, they added sweet and spicy red peppers to the king's leftover *soffritto* and invented the classic Neapolitan dish *zuppe di soffritto*. In the sixth century, the Lombard duke Arechi, who governed from Benevento for fifty years, divided his territory into *gastaldi,* giving the Gastoldato di Sant' Agata to his adopted sons, Grimoaldo and Rodoaldo. During their administration, the brothers were known to throw sumptuous outdoor banquets for local townspeople and the surrounding duchy, often lasting through the night. The royal Lombards set up kitchens in every piazza in Sant' Agata, with long tables displaying whole barrels of wine, large *l'ammulelle,* wine pitchers, and spreads of wild game dishes.

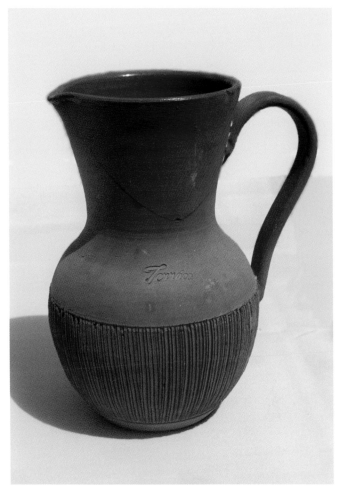

L'ammulella

Coniglio in Umido
Stewed Rabbit with Vegetables

SERVES 6
PREPARATION TIME: 1 HOUR

⅓ cup extra virgin olive oil

1 medium-sized rabbit, about 2½ pounds, cut into serving pieces

1 medium-sized onion, sliced or chopped

1 large celery stalk, cut into ½-inch dice

1 large carrot, peeled and cut into ½-inch dice

4 cloves garlic, coarsely chopped

½ cup dry white wine

Pinch of dried or chopped fresh rosemary

12 cherry tomatoes, slit and squeezed to expel seeds

Salt and freshly ground black pepper

Chicken broth or water, if needed

Heat oil until very hot in a large frying pan over medium heat. Add rabbit, onion, celery, carrot, and garlic and sauté, covered, for 10 to 15 minutes, stirring frequently, or until golden brown. Add white wine, rosemary, cherry tomatoes, and salt and pepper to taste. Give it a good stir and let the wine evaporate. If necessary, add enough chicken broth or water to keep moist. Cover and simmer for another 15 to 20 minutes, or until the rabbit is tender but still juicy. Season to taste with salt and pepper. Serve the rabbit with the vegetables and sauce in the pan.

'Zi Giuannina and Silvio Suppa

Chapter 3
'A Nonna's Apprentice

'A carn fà carn, 'U vin fà sang, 'A fatic fà iettà 'u sang.
Meat makes flesh, Wine makes blood, Work makes you sweat blood.

The story of this cookbook and how authentic Campanian cuisine was transported to the United States began in the early 1950s, when young Silvio Suppa became curious about his grandmother's old ways of cooking. Carmela Ianotta in Izzo, his maternal grandmother, was born in 1885, a southern farming woman full of common sense and motherliness who nurtured seven daughters, two sons, a husband, and a team of field hands who worked the family farm from dawn to dusk. Carmela inherited traditional ways of cooking from her mother, whose dishes

Silvio Suppa (standing) with the Suppa family.
Contrado Sanquinito, early 1950s. Suppa family archives

spanned back centuries. A tall, thin woman with a big heart, Carmela was known by all as *'Zi Minella*, Aunt Minella. After having seven daughters, and yearning for a son, she adopted a little boy she had breastfed from birth from a poor family who could no longer support him. She later had a son, Ginesio.

As a young boy, Silvio could often be found around his grandmother's kitchen. In a time before refrigerators, when Silvio came home from school, his first stop at grandmother's kitchen was always at *'a matarc*, a rectangular maple cabinet where she stored loaves of freshly baked bread and leftover *pasta e fasul* and *pacche e fasul* wrapped in linens.

Zuppa e Fasul
Bean Soup

SERVES 4
PREPARATION TIME: 2 DAYS

'A nonna, my grandmother, cooked on a *fornacella*, a southern Italian farmer's version of the modern range, made of brick and constructed in a square shape. It had a hole at the center with removable rings to adjust to different pot sizes. Beneath was a door where a fire was made from twigs and

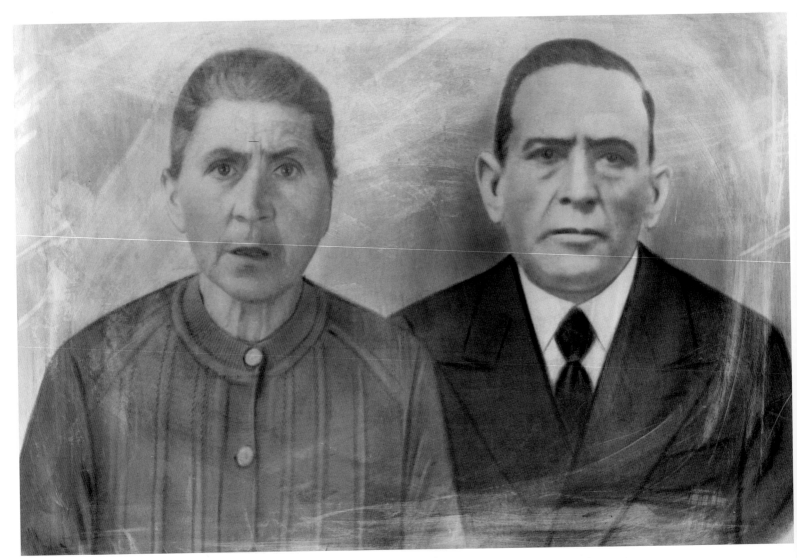

Carmela and Angelo Izzo

branches gathered from the fields. She also cooked at a fireplace, *'o fucular,* where *'a caurar,* a large copper pot, was hung from a chain over the fire. In the fireplace, cannellini beans, *fave,* and *ceci* were always being slow-cooked in the *pignáta,* a small clay pot with two handles, with pieces of *'a cótena,* the skin from the belly, ear, or foot of the pig, to give it flavor. My grandmother Carmela knew my favorite dish—*'a zuppa e fasul,* bean soup, a dish of hard, leftover bread covered with beans and raw onions and drizzled with local olive oil.

1 pound dried white cannellini beans

1 tablespoon salt

Freshly ground black pepper

4 thick slices crusty peasant bread, stale or toasted, or *viscuott**

¾ to 1 cup extra virgin olive oil

1 large red onion, cut into chunks

Wash beans and soak overnight in enough water to cover by 2 inches. Drain the beans and place in a pot. A *pignáta* is ideal but very difficult to find, even in Italy, so use whatever you have. Add enough water to cover by a few inches and salt. Place the pot over high heat and bring to a boil, then reduce the heat to low and simmer for approximately 1 hour, or until the beans are soft to the bite. (Always be sure the beans are covered with boiling water as they cook.) Season with salt and pepper to taste.

Place bread in each bowl. Ladle the beans over the bread, with enough cooking liquid to soak the bread. Drizzle with oil to taste and top with a few chunks of onion.

Note: Viscuott is the Neapolitan word the Sant' Agatese use for *biscotti,* or hard biscuits. Ring shaped and rectangular *freselle* and *taralli* are other common *biscotti* which can be peppery, seeded, or plain. *Biscotti* are widely-known as after dinner dessert cookies to complement expresso or cappuccino. The recipes in this book refer to *viscuott* or *biscotti,* the hard bread version and not the sweetened type. In Italian American communities, bakeries and grocers offer *freselle* and many forms of *biscotti.*

'A nonna enjoyed a wide variety of fresh herbs and vegetables from her *orto,* her garden, just outside her kitchen door—dandelions, chicory, basil, parsley, tomatoes, eggplants and peppers. We had *'u puzzo,* a well, nearby in the courtyard, which we used for household needs. We pulled the pails of water out with a rope that wound around a *vinnul',* a spool, and then we brought the water into the house to cook and to drink. Vegetables were washed two and three times at our *puzzo,* well, for her *menesta,* soups. We also had a well in the fields near the pumpkins and corn with a water wheel, *'u centimmolo,* which also was used to irrigate the *orto* and the rest

Pignáta

Green Benevento valley in the Campania region

of the farm and everything we had planted in the garden. On a well-worn path surrounding the *centimmolo* an ox, horse, or mule, blindfolded and attached to a pole with a harness, walked around and around, driving the mechanism to pull the water out of the well. It had a long chain of long *catose,* buckets, with a belt of buckets that went face down into the water and came up full, and as they turned they dumped the water into a chute that carried the water to a pool. From there a tube led the water out to all of the rows of corn. As each row was filled with enough water, a field hand on the other end of the row would call out, *"Gira l'acqua, gira amprèssa,"* Go on to the next one, hurry up.

At times she would make *menesta maritata,* married soup, with pork and beans, in a large pot over the fireplace. On the following day, leftover bread was put in a pot with oil and garlic, cherry peppers, and leftover *menesta.* The bread soaked up the oil, and the hearty dish was usually consumed the next morning for *colazione*, breakfast. *'A nonna* never wasted food and she used to make *fichi e mele secche*, dried apples, figs, and peppers too. She used to thread them together with a needle by hand and string and hang them like a beaded necklace along the side of the house to dry in the sun. When they were dry, she stored them away for the winter.

Within her home, in a cool section of the house, was the *granaio*, a storage room, constructed of wood—an Italian version of a silo—for storing wheat until it was brought to the *mulinaio*, the miller, to be ground into flour. The wheat in my grandmother's storage room was processed by age-old methods. Farmers cut the wheat with *'a falce*, a sickle, and tied it into bundles. Then they put the bundles into piles, *i pignun*, which were pointed upward so the rain slid straight down the sides and the wheat stayed dry. They left the wheat out for a few days, then they picked it up with the cart and carried it to the *mezz' all' aria*, the courtyard, where they threshed it with *'a trebbia*, the threshing machine.

In the stable the cows, tied by a rope, were fed in the *mangiatoia*, a long wooden box built into the wall running across the stable. We also grew *graurinio*, corn, as feed for the chickens, cows, horses, goats, and rabbits. We even had *i ciucci sardagnuoli*, a small, rare breed of donkeys; one we used to call "Carolina" and she answered us with a loud hee-haw! Our favorite cow was called "Zuccarella," the one who always plowed the land. As children we played with and talked to them—they were so well trained. We had turkeys, ducks, and pigeons too. We didn't have to go anywhere to buy anything—it was all there on our farm. Cows who had just given birth were used for milk, while others were yoked to the *aratro*, the plow, and they also pulled the *carretto*, a wagon, full of hay, greens, tools, and workers, back and forth from the fields. We had two oxen with a wooden *iulo* over the neck and a V-shaped piece of wood called a *paio*, the harness, pulling the *carro*, a big wagon used for carrying wheat, corn, and beans to the *mezz' all' aria*, the walled area of *tufo* paved with cobblestones where we processed all the dried *frumento*: the *grano*, wheat, *granturco*, corn, *biava*, oats, and *cicir*, chickpeas.

Out in the fields, the bean plants matured—*cicir*, fava, red and white cannellini beans (which were the most popular in our area), *barlotti* and *uocchio i pernice*, the eye-of-a-partridge beans, so named because they were small, *fasul neri*, black beans, and *fasul scritti*, beans that looked like someone had written on

them in purple ink. When the beans turned brown, they pulled the plants out and put them in sheets, tied the four ends of the sheets into big bundles, and the women carried them home on their heads. When they got home, they dumped them out in the middle of the *aia*, the area in the middle of the courtyard, where they processed the beans. They unwrapped the plants from the sheets and placed them in thin layers in the hot sun for four to five days, because the pods were still moist inside. They turned the plants in the sun each day until dry and brittle, at which point they were ready to be beaten and the shells broke easily so the beans fell out.

The way they processed beans went like this. Two people usually stood across from each other on either side of the bed of beans laid out in the *aia*. They worked and beat the beans with perfect timing, alternating and beating in rhythm with *'o vivill*, an older version of the American flail. *'O vivill* consisted of a four-foot-long stick that you held in your hands and a shorter, heavier, free-swinging stick attached by a piece of leather at the end. With a rolling outward motion from the chest, each person thwacked the dried bean plants in a rhythmic pounding, separating the dry brittle plant from the shells. They used to sing songs, *le canzioni folcloristiche*, folklore songs, while they worked. After the plants were beaten and all the beans were out of their shells, they went over everything with *'o rastiell*, a wooden rake with wide teeth. Once raked back and forth, *i streppun*, stalks, would separate and what was left was the beans and leftover shells. Then they made two piles. The stalks of the plants were fed to the cows and goats and sheep. The beans and shells were piled in the far corner of the *aia*, because you needed a lot of distance for the next step of the process.

This centuries-old way of separating the beans was done on windy, sunny days when the wind blew in the right direction and the air was dry. The beans and small twigs and shells were piled up in the opposite corner of the courtyard. Using a wide wooden square shovel, *'a pala per auriá*, and with great skill, they threw the beans twenty to twenty-five feet, using the exact force and turning the shovel in a method known as *auriá*, twisting it as they heaved it in the air with perfect timing to separate the light debris from the heavier beans. The lighter debris fell short, and the beans, because of their weight, hit the walls of the far corner of the courtyard and fell into a pile. With the beans separated, they put them in sacks and brought them to the *granaio*.

Zuppa di Fave
Fava Bean Soup

SERVES 4 TO 6
PREPARATION TIME: 30 TO 40 MINUTES

⅓ cup extra virgin olive oil

4 ounces end or scrap piece of prosciutto, coarsely chopped

8 cloves garlic, lightly smashed with your hand or a kitchen utensil, peel discarded

2 celery stalks, cut crosswise into ½-inch slices

2 pounds shelled fresh fava beans

½ cup dry white wine

About 2 cups chicken broth or water

Salt and freshly ground black pepper

Peperoncino (crushed dried hot red pepper), optional

Heat olive oil in a large pot over medium heat. Add prosciutto and cook, stirring for approximately 2 minutes, or until crispy. Add garlic and cook until blond in color. Add celery and fava beans. Add white wine and continue to cook, stirring for 4 minutes, or until the wine has evaporated. Add enough chicken broth or water to cover contents, and salt and pepper to taste. Let simmer for 15 to 20 minutes, or until fava beans are tender. Give a final taste for seasoning, adding peperoncino (crushed dried hot red pepper) if you wish. Serve in a deep bowl over stale or toasted peasant bread, *freselle*, or *viscuott*, hard bread biscuits.

'A Menesta Ammaritata
Mixed Meat and Greens Soup

SERVES 10 TO 12
PREPARATION TIME: 2 TO 4 HOURS

Ideal parts for this recipe are ribs, shanks, and cut prosciutto, pigs feet, *cotica*, pigs ears, and leftover bone of prosciutto. Use your judgment according to availability and your liking. The first set of ingredients are up-to-date and available; the second are traditional and harder to find.

4 pounds beef and pork

5 quarts water

6 cloves garlic

3 celery stalks

Salt

5 pounds mixed greens: chicory, Napa cabbage, Savoy cabbage, Tuscan kale, Swiss chard, escarole

Peperoncino (crushed dried hot red pepper)

½ cup extra virgin olive oil

In a large stockpot, combine the meats, water, garlic, celery stalks, and some salt. Simmer over medium heat for approximately 1 to 3 hours, frequently skimming fat and foam off the top, or until the meat is completely tender. Take the meat out of the broth and set aside. Add all greens, washed and drained, to the broth and cook for approximately 30 minutes, or until they are tender but still retain their shape. Give a final taste for salt and add hot red pepper to taste. Return the meat to the pot. The meat and greens should be nearly covered by the broth; add more water if needed. Simmer for 5 minutes, then remove from the heat and let sit for 15 minutes before serving. Ladle broth, meat, and greens into each bowl. Serve with slices of crusty peasant bread and drizzle with the olive oil.

Because of the long process of this recipe, I suggest cooking the meats the day before. On the next day, cook the greens in the broth and complete the recipe.

'A menesta ammaritata

Chapter 4
My First Dishes

Mazz e panell, fanno i figli bell,
Pane senza mazz, fann i figli pazz.
Bread and the paddle make good children,
Bread without the paddle makes bad children.

Silvio's chance to learn traditional ways of Campanian cooking by observing his grandmother as she prepared dishes from memorized heirloom recipes came when his mother was bedridden with serious arthritis. His interest in the healing power of natural, unprocessed foods deepened as he watched his sixty-five-year-old grandmother nurse his mother back to health with nutritious soups. After his father and brothers returned home from work, Silvio, being the youngest of the family, assumed more cooking responsibilities in the kitchen while Carmela tended to his mother.

Silvio's first experience cooking alongside his grandmother was making chicken soup. After his grandmother killed the chicken, she plucked the feathers and singed it over the fire to clean it. She sent him to pick celery, basil, tomatoes, baby onions, carrots, and parsley from the garden just outside the kitchen. As she cut the chicken, she asked her grandson to get water, wash the pots, cut the carrots and celery, and wash the vegetables in preparation for the soup. In a separate pot, water was made ready for *pastina e stellucce*, little star pasta, or *acini di pepe*, orzo, which was added to the soup. The broth simmered slowly for two to three hours, sending a delicious aroma wafting through the household. Years later in America, Silvio continued making his grandmother's chicken soup for his three sons—Ilario, Giuseppe, and Antonio—when they asked "Doctor Papa" to make it for them when they were sick.

Ravello on the Amalfi Coast (right)

Brodino di Pollo
Chicken Soup

SERVES 6

PREPARATION TIME: 2 HOURS

5 quarts water

One 3- to 4-pound chicken, cut into quarters

2 large celery stalks, cut crosswise into 1-inch pieces

2 large carrots, peeled, split in half lengthwise, and cut crosswise into ½-inch pieces

1 small onion, cut into quarters

2 medium-sized fresh tomatoes, halved, squeezed to expel seeds, and coarsely chopped

6 sprigs Italian parsley

8 large leaves fresh basil

Salt and freshly ground black pepper

1 pound pastina (*stellucce, orzo, acini di pepe*)

In a large pot, combine all ingredients except the pasta, adding salt and pepper to taste. Bring to a boil, then adjust the heat and simmer for 1½ to 2 hours, periodically skimming the foam off the top, until the chicken is cooked and comes off the bone easily. Remove from the heat. Take the chicken out of the pot and pick the meat from the bones, discarding the bones and skin. Return the meat to the broth. In a separate pot, cook the pastina in boiling salted water according to the directions on the package. Drain and add to the soup. Over medium heat, bring the soup to a boil, then remove from the heat immediately. Ladle the soup into bowls and serve.

While working alongside her in the kitchen, Silvio noticed that his grandmother never followed precise measurements or exact steps from any written recipes. Ever curious about her techniques and wanting to learn the secrets of good cooking, he asked how much of each ingredient was needed as she made soups and sauces. Carmela finally answered her grandson's questions in terms as simple and straightforward as her dishes.

"Put this much," she told me, and she showed me what she was adding to the broth. She said, "*Mett nu poc e chest' e nu' poc e chell.*" (Put a little bit of this and a little bit of that.) So then I asked, "*'A nonna, che altro ci mett a dint?*" (Grandma, what else should we put in?) And she answered, "*Quando fai 'a salsa, quando fai 'o brodo, chella che ci mett a dint', chella ci trovi.' A te che ti piace? A gallina? Allora, ci mett a gallina! Se ti piace carne di maiale, allora ci mett maiale. Chella che ci mett a dint', chella che ci trovi!*" (When you make a sauce or a soup, whatever you put into it, that's what you'll get out of it. So what do you like? Chicken? Then put in chicken! If you like pork, put in pork. Whatever you put in, that's what you'll find!)

The first dish I cooked by myself, the one I learned from my grandmother, which was her favorite, was *Spaghetti ca Pummaròla Sciué-Sciué*, spaghetti with a quick tomato sauce made fresh right from the garden. As we were picking ripe plum tomatoes, garlic, and basil from the garden, she used to say to me, "*'A vasenicòla e pummaròla vanno assieme come marito e muglièra,*"—basil and tomato go together like husband and wife. Then she'd take a pinch of oregano and some extra virgin olive oil, and put a pot on the fireplace hearth, covering the bottom with the oil. When the oil was hot, she added a dozen garlic cloves and told me one of her cooking secrets. Instead of cutting the garlic with a knife, she used a different method. So I asked, "*Nonna, perché non usa 'o coltello?*" (Grandmother, why don't you use a knife?) And she answered, "*No, no è uguale, piglia l'aglio e acciaccà con la mano e mett subito subito in da l'uóglio, cosi non perde 'o sapore!*" (No, it's not the same when you use a knife. Take the garlic and smash it on the counter with your hands and put it right into the oil, that way it won't lose its flavor.)

Grandmother Carmela's tianella i creta

Spaghetti ca pummaròla sciué-sciué

Then she taught me the art of preparing fresh San Marzano plum tomatoes. She showed me how to squeeze them under water with the index finger and the thumb so that the seeds would not splash all over. Then she showed me how to break them apart with both hands and put them in a container until I was finished. Then she removed the pot from the heat so that the hot oil would not splatter and added the tomatoes, spices, and herbs to the sizzling oil and golden cooked garlic. Finally, she added fresh basil, oregano, and salt. She cooked the sauce for only ten minutes to preserve its freshness and natural flavors.

Spaghetti ca Pummaròla Sciué-Sciué
Spaghetti with Quick Tomato Sauce

SERVES 4
PREPARATION TIME: 20 MINUTES

⅓ cup extra virgin olive oil

4 cloves garlic, lightly smashed with your hand or a kitchen utensil, peel discarded

2 pounds ripe plum tomatoes, halved, squeezed to expel the seeds, and chopped or torn in pieces

Pinch of dried oregano

1 cup fresh basil leaves, torn

Salt and freshly ground black pepper

1 pound spaghetti, preferably imported from Italy

In a medium-sized pot, preferably terracotta, heat oil over medium heat. Add garlic and sauté until golden. Add tomatoes and cook for approximately 10 minutes, or until tomatoes have softened and released their juice but still retain some of their shape. Add oregano, half of the basil, and salt and pepper to taste. Cook for 1 minute and then set aside.

Cook pasta in a pot of boiling salted water following instructions on the package. Drain, return to the pot, and add the sauce, reheated if necessary. Toss well and serve immediately in pasta bowls. Garnish with the rest of the basil.

As Silvio was spending more and more time by his grandmother's side, Carmela decided to play a trick on her young apprentice.

One day we were picking hot peppers together in the garden, and she said to me, "Silvio, try this pepper, it's good!" So I took a bite out of it and it immediately burned my mouth. I ran out for water! With a slight grin on her face, she said, *"Eh, bella a nonna, tu t'adda imparà tutta cosa, eppure chiste 'ccà so buon, pure i' stonco ancora imparando a fa a mangia!"* (Grandmother loves you, but you have to learn everything about cooking. Even I am still learning how to cook!)

Children and fountain in the town square of Bitonto, Puglie

Chapter 5

’A Marenna on the Farm

Meglio un uovo oggi che una gallina domani.
Better to have an egg today than a chicken tomorrow.

My grandmother used to prepare *’a marenna,* a dry meal for the workers in the field and family around nine o’clock in the morning. She made frittatas, or omelets, with whatever was available—with *cucuzzo e cipolla,* potatoes and onions, or squash and onions, or *i sparaci,* with asparagus. Sometimes for her omelet she picked *tavarini,* a rare plant from the asparagus family yet leafy around the trunk. She used to find them at the foot of the hills, along with *viticelle,* wild vines, that climbed on the trees. She picked only the tender tops of the vines; they were bitter and had to be blanched, drained, and then fried. Sometimes she made fried peppers and potatoes, or she brought homemade cheeses and *supressata,* sausage. She always brought *’o paniell’ e pan,* a loaf of bread, which was usually corn and wheat bread. They used cornmeal because it kept the bread moist gave it a longer life before going stale. She made twelve loaves the size of steering wheels every week.

After everything was ready, my grandmother took *’o cuofano,* a huge wicker basket, and she placed the bread, the omelets, checkered tablecloths, and utensils in it. Then she made *’o truocchio,* rolling an old tablecloth or scarf into a thin long line and then coiling it like a snake, passing the loose end through the center to lock the whole thing securely so it wouldn’t come apart. She put *’o truocchio* on her head to hold the basket in place, lifted her filled basket and placed it on her head, grabbed a gallon of wine, and, leaving one hand free, walked out to the fields. I used to walk with her and she walked really straight, even through the rough terrain of the fields, with the basket perfectly balanced on her head, where she would meet my grandfather and his crew, including the family. Even though she was totally loaded down, she’d worry about me falling, and she’d say to me, *“Va chianu chian, a bella nonna”*—walk slow, grandmother loves you.

'A Frittat chi Sparaci
Asparagus Frittata

SERVES 2 TO 8
PREPARATION TIME: 20 MINUTES

1 bunch asparagus, approximately 12 ounces

¼ cup extra virgin olive oil

4 large eggs

4 heaping tablespoons grated parmigiano cheese

Salt and freshly ground black pepper

Preheat the oven to 375 degrees. Snap off and discard the woody bottoms of the asparagus stalks and break the tender parts into 2-inch pieces. Heat the oil in a medium-sized non-stick omelet pan over medium heat. Add the asparagus and cook, stirring frequently, until tender. In a bowl, beat the eggs, cheese, and a pinch each of salt and pepper until well mixed. Add the egg mixture to the asparagus and spread it evenly over the top. Bake the frittata for 5 to 8 minutes, depending on thickness. When ready, the frittata should be firm and light brown in color. You can serve the frittata upside down—invert a dish over the pan, hold both, and flip over—or you can use a spatula to slide it onto a serving dish. The second option is a bit easier. Cut the frittata into as many slices as you like, just like pizza. Serve immediately or enjoy later at room temperature or even the next day, cold out of the refrigerator.

Frittata chi Patan e Cipolla
Potatoes and Onion Frittata

SERVES 4 TO 6
PREPARATION TIME: ½ HOUR

¼ cup extra virgin olive oil

1 small onion, chopped

2 medium-sized potatoes, peeled and cut into ½-inch cubes

4 large eggs

½ cup fresh Italian parsley, chopped

¼ cup grated parmigiano cheese

Salt and freshly ground black pepper

'A frittat chi sparaci

Preheat the oven to 375 degrees. Heat the oil in a medium-sized nonstick omelet pan over medium heat. Add onions and potatoes and cook for approximately 10 minutes, stirring constantly to prevent sticking, until the vegetables are tender but retain their shape. In a bowl, thoroughly beat the eggs, half of the parsley, cheese, and salt and pepper to taste. Pour the egg mixture evenly over the potatoes and onions. Let cook for 1 minute, then bake for 5 to 8 minutes, or until puffy and firm. Flip or slide onto a round plate, slice as you like, and sprinkle the rest of the parsley over it. Serve hot, at room temperature, or cold out of the refrigerator the next day.

Frittata chi Cucuzzielli e Cipolla
Zucchini and Onion Frittata

SERVES 2 TO 8
PREPARATION TIME: 30 MINUTES

¼ cup extra virgin olive oil

1 small onion, sliced

2 small zucchini about 6 ounces each, halved lengthwise, then cut crosswise into ¼-inch half-moons

Salt and freshly ground black pepper

4 large eggs

¼ cup grated parmigiano cheese

½ cup chopped fresh Italian parsley

Preheat the oven to 375 degreees. In a medium-sized non-stick omelet pan, heat the oil over medium heat. Add the onion and let cook for 2 to 3 minutes, or until slightly softened. Add the zucchini and cook for an additional 3 to 4 minutes, stirring frequently. Add a pinch each of salt and pepper. In a bowl, beat the eggs, cheese, and half of the parsley. Pour the egg mixture evenly over the zucchini and onions. Let cook for 1 minute, then bake for 5 to 8 minutes, or until puffy and firm. Flip or slide onto a round plate, slice as you like, and sprinkle the rest of the parsley over it. Serve hot, at room temperature, or cold out of the refrigerator the next day.

Sciurilli 'Mbuttinat ca' Ricott
Stuffed Squash Flowers with Ricotta

SERVES 4
PREPARATION TIME: 30 TO 45 MINUTES

1¼ cups ricotta

¼ cup grated parmigiano cheese

3 large eggs

Salt and freshly ground black pepper

12 large squash flowers

¾ cup vegetable oil for frying

1 cup all-purpose flour

6 sprigs Italian parsley or basil

In a bowl, mix the ricotta, grated cheese, 1 egg, and a pinch each of salt and pepper. Open a flower, hold it in one hand, and with the other hand spoon the ricotta mixture into the flower without breaking it. Repeat until all the flowers are stuffed. Heat the oil in a medium-sized frying pan over medium heat. In a shallow bowl, beat 2 eggs with a pinch each of salt and pepper. Roll each flower in flour and then dip in the beaten eggs. Lay them carefully in the hot oil and cook on both sides to a nice gold color. Lay them on paper towels to drain. Arrange them on a nice serving plate and garnish with parsley or basil sprigs.

Tianella i creta

Chapter 6

Il Pranzo on the Farm

Te mangi sta menesta, O te vutti da sta finèsta.

Either eat this soup, or go out through the window.

After '*a marènna*, my grandmother went back to the house to start preparing for *il pranzo*, which was eaten around one o'clock in the afternoon. On the return from the fields, she'd pick some grass, make big bundles, and feed it to the animals—the pigs, the cows. She'd stop in the *orto*, the garden right behind the house, and pick hot cherry peppers, scallions, onions, eggplants, basil, and other herbs—that was her shopping place on the way home. The afternoon meal was hot, with pasta and '*a secondo*, the second dish: fried peppers and potatoes; some pork meat; fried eggplant *fungitiello*, cut into cubes, with fresh tomatoes and herbs; or eggplant parmigiana. Some days, instead of pasta she brought out '*a menesta* with pigs' feet or ears or '*a menesta abbuscata cu l'uoss' di prusutt'*, a soup with five or six types of wild field greens—*cardilli, cicoria,* Italian dandelion, *scasseller,* and *rapest',* wild broccoli rabe—cooked with prosciuitto bones (after the meat was eaten), the end piece of the prosciutto, and the skin, '*a cótena.*

'A Menesta Abbuscata cu L'Uoss' i Prusutt'

Minestra with Prosciutto Bones

SERVES 4 TO 6

PREPARATION TIME: 1 HOUR

2 pounds mixed greens (escarole, chicory, dandelion) and/or broccoli rabe

⅔ cup extra virgin olive oil

Campania countryside

1 prosciutto bone, broken in two with a cleaver, or 8
  ounce scrap piece of prosciutto, cut into 6 to 8 pieces

6 cloves garlic lightly smashed with your hand or a
  kitchen utensil, peel discarded

½ cup dry white wine

2 cups cooked white cannellini beans, or 20 ounces
  undrained canned

Salt and freshly ground black pepper

2 cups chicken broth or water, hot

6 slices crusty peasant bread, toasted or stale

Remove any especially thick stems from the greens and wash well; place in a colander to drain. Heat ⅓ cup of the olive oil in a large pot over medium heat. Add the prosciutto and garlic and cook until the garlic is golden. Add the greens and white wine and cook, covered, for about 2 to 3 minutes. Take the cover off, stir the contents, and cook for another 3 to 4 minutes until the greens are well mixed and wilted. Add beans, salt and pepper to taste, and enough hot chicken broth or water to nearly cover the contents. Simmer until greens are tender but still retain their shape. Taste for salt and pepper. Remove from the heat and set aside. Put a slice of toasted or hard bread into each soup bowl. Discard any bones, ladle the soup into each bowl, and drizzle with the remaining olive oil.

Optional: If you prefer it hot and spicy, add peperoncino (crushed dried hot red pepper). Most of my family, especially 'Zi Ginesio, liked this dish hot and spicy, and my grandmother always sautéed a few pickled hot cherry peppers, stemmed and coarsely chopped, and poured them over each serving. Consider trying this.

Afternoon pranzo with the Suppa family

Cardilli e Fasul
Cardilli and Beans

Cardilli is a wild field green native to Campania. It is closest to the wild American dandelion.

SERVES 4 TO 6

PREPARATION TIME: 1 HOUR

2 pounds cardilli or dandelions

⅔ cup extra virgin olive oil

3 to 4 ounces end or scrap piece of prosciutto, cut into 3 or 4 pieces

6 cloves garlic, lightly smashed with your hand or a kitchen utensil, peel discarded

½ cup dry white wine

2 cups cooked white cannellini beans, or 20 ounces undrained canned

Salt and freshly ground black pepper

2 cups chicken broth or water, hot

6 slices crusty peasant bread, toasted or stale

Wash and drain the greens. Heat ⅓ cup of the olive oil in a large pot over medium heat. Add the prosciutto and garlic and cook until both turn crispy and the garlic is golden. Add the greens and wine and cook, covered, for about 2 to 3 minutes. Remove the cover, stir the contents, and let cook for another 3 to 4 minutes until the greens are well mixed and wilted. Add beans, salt and pepper to taste, and enough hot chicken broth or water to nearly cover the contents. Simmer until greens are tender but still retain their shape. Add salt and pepper to taste. Remove from the heat and set aside. Put a slice of toasted or hard bread in each soup bowl. Ladle the soup into each bowl and drizzle with the remaining olive oil. If you prefer it hot and spicy, add peperoncino (crushed dried hot red pepper).

My grandmother's original recipe called for pigs' feet. If you want to try them, prepare this recipe with dried cannellini beans and cook the feet with the beans. She also sautéed a few pickled hot cherry peppers, stemmed and coarsely chopped, and poured them over each serving.

Sunny afternoon in Sant' Agata de' Goti

Chapter 7

La Cena on the Farm

Ammo fernuto a tarallucci e vino.
We had a beautiful ending to our day.

The evening meal, the *cena,* was usually light. The big meal was always at midday. My grandmother would have a fire constantly going in the fireplace until we went to sleep. At night the men would gather around the fire. They used to drink what they called *orzo,* especially during the war and after because there wasn't much coffee and it was very expensive. *Orzo* is barley, a grain similar to wheat. The barley was picked after the flowers and stems matured and dried. Then it was put through *'a trebbia,* a thresher, to separate the grain from the straw. We kept some for ourselves, which we roasted it in the fireplace in a homemade roasting pan. The rest was stored in large burlap sacks and sold to townspeople who came around and bought it or was fed to the animals. My grandmother always brewed it at night because it was like our chamomile tea: it had no caffeine and helped us sleep. My grandmother ground the *orzo* with a handmade hand grinder; it had a handle that turned and a box on the bottom to catch the ground *orzo.* She boiled water in the fireplace and then she put a linen cloth over the top of the pot, put the *orzo* on the linen, like a coffee filter, poured boiling water over it, and the brewed *orzo* dripped slowly into the pot.

At night, while we drank the *orzo* and everyone gathered around the heat of the fireplace, most of the time my grandmother came out with homemade cookies or *biscotti,* biscuits, or *taralli,* ring-shaped biscuits, to go with it. I remember how the women stayed back from the fire because they said the heat made their legs ugly with *i ruazz,* a ruddy color from being too close to the flames. To entertain themselves at night, they used to tell all kinds of stories. My Uncle Ginesio used to tell us the story "The Prisoner and the Sack." It was a story to teach children to use their wits in certain situations, and to entertain us, too.

The story went something like this:

(left) Wine and taralli, Café Allegre

The Prisoner and the Sack

In the old days, it was the custom that when the people saw the king or the queen, they genuflected in their honor. But one day this young man in the town saw the king pass by and refused to recognize him and would not genuflect. When the king found out, he ordered his royal guards to seize the man and bring him to the castle to be punished. So the guards faithfully followed the orders of the king, found the young man, placed him in a big sack, and tied the top so he couldn't escape. On the way to the castle the guards stopped at a *taverna*, a small restaurant, to buy some wine and have something to eat. They put the sack against the entrance door, then went to eat their meal. While they were eating, a man entered the *taverna* and saw the sack with something moving inside. He heard someone talking and asked, "Who's in there and what are you saying?" The young man inside cleverly said, "I can't believe they captured me and they want to take me to the king because he wants me to marry his daughter and I don't want to do that." He seemed terrified at the thought from inside the sack. So the man said to him, "Why don't I free you and I'll get into the sack? Then I can marry the king's daughter." So they exchanged places—the young man got out, tied the other up, and, as if nothing had happened, ran away as fast as he could. When the guards finished their meal, they took the sack, thinking they had their man, and headed for the castle. They brought the man in the sack to the king and they were ordered by the king to lay the man out and give him a beating for being disrespectful and to then let him go. The guards followed the king's order and beat the man, but the disrespectful young man had gotten away, laughing all the way home.

Orecchiette Sant' Agatese
Little Ear Pasta Sant' Agatese Style

SERVES 4 TO 6
PREPARATION TIME: 30 MINUTES

This dish is very well known around Sant' Agata, a town near where I grew up, and one I still love. The recipe was used frequently during *stagione dei zucchini*, zucchini season, when my grandmother's *orto*, her vegetable garden, was abundant with *pomodorini*, cherry tomatoes, and basil. My grandmother used to come out of the *orto* with her *'o sinat*, a white apron, which she used like a big pouch to gather vegetables. She filled it up with zucchini, basil, *pomodorini*, and green onions for that night's *cena*. Instead of going shopping at a store, she'd go right to the *orto* to pick whatever she needed fresh for that night and come into the house and put it all on the table. Then she'd wash and dry all the vegetables and start her setup for dinner. Then my grandfather Angelo, when he came home from working in the fields, used to say to me, "*Silvio assettata, facimm' nu' spuntino cu nu' bicchiere e vino assieme con me*"—Silvio, come and sit down and have a snack and a glass of wine with me. Then he would tell me stories about his life in America, and how he lived on Liberty Avenue with his sister Cuncetta in Brooklyn in 1901.

⅓ cup extra virgin olive oil

½ onion, finely chopped

4 slices prosciutto ⅛-inch thick, cut into julienne strips

2 small zucchini (about 6 ounces each), trimmed and thinly sliced

1 pound ripe cherry tomatoes, halved and squeezed to expel the seeds

1 cup fresh basil leaves, torn

Salt and freshly ground black pepper

1 pound orecchiette, preferably imported from Italy

Heat salted water for pasta in a medium-sized pot. Meanwhile, heat the oil in a large frying pan over medium heat. Add the onions and prosciutto and cook, stirring for approximately 5 minutes, or until the onions are translucent. Add the zucchini, tomatoes, half of the basil, and some salt and pepper. Cook for approximately 10 more minutes, or until the zucchini are tender and the tomatoes soft. Season with salt and pepper to your liking. Remove from the heat and set aside.

In the boiling water, cook the pasta following the directions on the package for *al dente*. Drain, reserving some of the cooking water. Add the zucchini mixture to the pasta and stir. If it looks too dry, add some of the pasta water (it should be moist but not soupy). Ladle pasta into each bowl, garnish generously with the remaining basil, and serve hot.

Chef Silvio cooking strangolaprievete

Strangolaprievete 'ru Cafon

Peasant Style
Priest-Strangler Macaroni

SERVES 4 TO 6

PREPARATION TIME: 35 MINUTES

As children we used to ask our parents why this pasta was called *strangolaprievete*, priest strangler. Being close to the church and the local priest, we thought it was a strange name. We all knew the local priest, Father Domenico Marciano. He was a *diocesi*, a parish priest, and we called him "Don Mimi." He ran the church of San Michele Archangelo in the nearby Contrada di Capitone, and he managed the church property, including farmland that he rented to farmers to pay for the expenses of the church. He had a *società* for young people, and he built a soccer field. The altar boys who served Mass played on the team, and they went on trips to Fatima and Montevergine. He also helped students having a hard time with school, tutoring them, and they in turn served Mass, which kept the community religious. Our parents told us the story that started, "*Si, ci steva 'na volta*"—Yes, once upon a time, this is what happened. And they told us that in Sant' Agata there once was a priest who loved this macaroni dish and ate so much that he choked to death on it, so they named it "*strangolaprievete*," priest-strangler macaroni.

    ¼ cup extra virgin olive oil

    ½ onion, finely chopped

    1 pound fresh Italian sausage without casing

    3 cups Chef Silvio's Sunday Sauce (see page 101),
        or your favorite pasta sauce

    1 cup fresh basil leaves, torn

    Salt and freshly ground black pepper

    1 pound *strangolaprievete* "priest-strangler" pasta or
        fusilli, if easier to find

    1 cup grated pecorino romano cheese

Heat salted water for pasta in a medium-sized pot. In another medium-sized pot, heat oil over medium heat. Add the sausage and onions and cook, breaking the sausage apart with a wooden spoon, until the onions are tender and the sausage loses its raw look, about 10 minutes. Add the sauce and half of the basil, stir well, and simmer for 5 minutes. Season to taste with salt and pepper. Remove from the heat and set aside.

In the pot of boiling water, cook the pasta following the directions on the package for *al dente*. Drain, reserving some of the cooking water. Add three-quarters of the sauce to the pasta along with half of the grated cheese; stir well. If the pasta appears dry, add some of the pasta water. Ladle into serving bowls. Top with the rest of the sauce and cheese, garnish with the rest of the basil, and serve hot.

Strangolaprievete

Broccoli Rape con Salsiccia
Broccoli Rabe and Sausage

SERVES 4 TO 6

PREPARATION TIME: 30 MINUTES

2 bunches broccoli rabe, tough ends trimmed off

½ cup extra virgin olive oil

1 pound Italian sausage, cut into 1 inch pieces

8 cloves garlic, lightly smashed with your hand or a
    kitchen utensil, peel discarded

Salt and freshly ground black pepper

Peperoncino (crushed dried hot red pepper), optional

Boil broccoli rabe in a large pot of salted boiling water, making sure it is completely submerged, until tender, about 10 minutes. Drain, reserving 2 cups of the cooking water. Heat oil in a large frying pan over medium heat. Add the sausage and cook, stirring frequently to prevent sticking, until the sausage is crispy. Add garlic and cook until blond in color. Off the heat, add the broccoli rabe to the sausage. Return to the heat, add salt, black pepper, and peperoncino (crushed dried hot red pepper) to taste, and cook until sizzling. Give it a good stir and add enough broccoli cooking water to make juicy. With a pair of tongs, transfer everything onto one big plate (for family style) or to individual plates. Pour pan juices evenly over each dish. Serve with toasted crusty peasant bread.

Broccoli rape con salsiccia

Chapter 8
Shepherd Dishes

Shepherds in farming settlements around Sant' Agata raised and tended their flocks in much the same way as their Samnite forbearers had. Shepherds and farmers still abided by the season known as *'o fatto dei quattro aprilanti*, a dangerous time of unpredictable weather during the first four days of April. The end of March was usually difficult for shepherds, whose flocks had been confined close to home during the winter months with little to eat because of the cold weather. Often desperate and in fear of losing their precious herds, they waited with great anticipation for the passing of the first four days of April and the return of favorable weather to move their flocks from the protection of their barns to the verdant feeding slopes in the mountains of Taburno.

Ancient oral tradition among shepherds, steeped in Campanian folk mythology with Greek-like gods, tells the cautionary tale of one shepherd who failed to abide by the *'o fatto dei quattro aprilanti*. On March 30, the weather seemed good enough to move his flock to the hills, and with the hubris of a tragic Greek hero, he foolishly sang a defiant song out to the god of March: *"Marzo, marzecchia / I pecorelle mie hanno cacciato tutti i cornecchie"* (March, Marchecchi / The little horns of my young sheep are starting to come out), meaning that his sheep were getting bigger, April was just around the corner, and there was nothing to worry about for the rest of the year. When March heard the

(left) Sheep in the hills of Benevento

shepherd's song, he became furious and asked his brother April for vengeance in a short rhyme: *"Aprile mio fratello / prestami quatto giornatelle / perchè aggia ammazzà / sti quatt' pecorelle"* (My brother April / Let me borrow four short days / Because I must kill / these four little sheep). April agreed to his brother March's request and granted March control over the weather for first four days of April, *"I quattro aprilanti."* March, with Zeus-like anger and fury, hurled a thunderous *tempesta*, a storm with heavy hailstorms that lasted the first four days of April, killing the shepherd's young sheep, which were left stranded in the mountains with no protection. Shepherds in the contradas around Sant'Agata still recite the story of March's wrath and the shepherd's punishment for not abiding by the seasons, and they keep their flocks close to home in the *stalla*, the barn, until the passing of the *'o fatto dei quattro aprilanti.*

In the springtime, after the long winter, they cut the *pecore*, the sheep's thick coats that had grown over the winter, with special scissors to get bales of wool, and they'd put them in big burlap sacks and linen sheets. The shepherds sold the wool to merchants who came with trucks, mostly wool manufacturers from northern Italy, and they brought it back to their factories to make suits and sweaters. After the sheep gave birth, they were milked morning and night. Some shepherds made pecorino cheese from milk and some sold the milk they didn't need to *'o lattaro*, the milkman, who used to come with a truck with a tank on it. And we used to carry the milk in *secchi*, covered pails, filling them with the extra sheep's milk we had left over from cheese making. We walked to the street at the time the *lattaro* passed by and handed it to him. He measured the milk with his own measuring pail, and marked down how many liters on our *cartella*, our weekly card. At the end of the week, he totaled it all up and paid us.

During winters the flocks stayed on the plains and were fed hay. Summers were spent in the hills. Once the weather got better, the shepherds took their sheep to graze in the mountains, whistling as they went along to the sheepdogs to direct the flocks. They carried with them a *reta*, a holding pen constructed of posts and thin ropes made by *'o funaro*, the ropemaker, from the *canapa* stalks that were cultivated around Naples and grew tall like sunflowers in the fields. When the shepherds were in the hills or on the plains, the wooden posts attached to the ropes could be rolled out for use and then rolled back up into bundles when the flock was ready to move on. The shepherds used *'o maglio*, a hand-made wooden sledgehammer, which had a hollowed spot in the middle of the head so that when it struck the fence

Sippiciano, Campania

Mount Taburno (right)

posts it would hit them squarely and bang them into the ground. When they unrolled 'a reta at the end of the day, it went around and around to make the makeshift holding pen for nighttime. The sheepdogs stayed close by to watch out for wolves who roved the mountains at night. While in the mountains, shepherds slept in 'o pagliaro, a three-walled hut similar to an Indian tent, made of woven straw and held up by posts, with an opening for them to crawl into at night. They lit a little fire outside to warm up and to cook. While they slept, the sheepdogs stayed vigilant, watching for wolves. After the sheep had grazed for two or three days, the shepherds would break down the walls of their straw hut, put it on the backs of their donkeys, roll up the reta, put it on their shoulders, and then move on to the next verdant location to feed the flocks of around two hundred sheep. Shepherds drove flocks this way for weeks at a time and sometimes they returned to rest at their base, their stalla, the barn, near the house if they weren't too far away.

On a visit to the Antonio Della Ratta Cheese Store in Sant' Agata, we met Alphonsina Della Ratta, who showed us how they still made a wide variety of goat and sheep cheeses following traditional ways. Her husband Antonio and brother-in-law Raffaele often brought their herds to the rugged terrain of Mount Taburno where they fed on l'erba medica, medicinal grasses believed to have curative properties, the secret of their flavorful cheeses.

Formaggio Fresco Pecorino e Uove Fritt'
Fried Eggs and Fresh Basket Cheese

SERVES 3
PREPARATION TIME: 15 MINUTES

½ cup extra virgin olive oil

3 large eggs

8 ounces fresh basket pecorino cheese, or fresh mozzarella cheese, cut in 3 slices

Salt and freshly ground black pepper

3 thick slices crusty Italian bread

Heat ¼ cup of the oil in a frying pan over medium heat. Break the eggs into the frying pan, without breaking the yolks. When the whites are cooked but the yolks still soft, take the eggs out with a spatula and place each one on a separate dish. Add the rest of oil to the pan. Lay the slices of cheese in the pan and sear on both sides. Take them out and place them next to the eggs. Salt and pepper the cheese and eggs. Now sear the bread in the pan on both sides until crispy and serve with the cheese and eggs. Enjoy nice and hot.

Pizza Rustica cu' cas i pecur
Spaghetti Pie with Pecorino Cheese

SERVES 4
PREPARATION TIME: 25 MINUTES

3 large eggs, lightly beaten

⅔ cup grated pecorino romano cheese

⅓ cup heavy cream

1 tablespoon chopped fresh Italian parsley

Salt and freshly ground black pepper

12 ounces cooked spaghetti, cold

2 tablespoons butter

5 ounces fresh basket pecorino cheese, or fresh goat cheese, sliced ¼-inch thick

3 ounces prosciutto, cut into strips, optional

In a bowl, beat the eggs, grated cheese, cream, parsley, and salt and pepper to taste until well combined. Stir in the spaghetti, then set aside. Place the butter in a non-stick baking pan or deep pie tin, melt the butter in a 450 degree oven, and spread over the pan bottom. Pour half of the spaghetti mixture into the buttered pan and spread evenly, then top evenly with the sliced cheese. Pour the rest of the spaghetti mixture over the top. Bake at 450 degrees for approximately 8 to 10 minutes, or until it is firm and golden. Cut into as many pieces as you like and serve hot, or refrigerate and serve cold over the next few days. Either way is delicious!

Optional: You can add prosciutto to this recipe either by stirring it into the spaghetti mixture or by laying it in an even layer over the cheese.

Alphonsina Della Ratta and Silvio Suppa at the Antonio Della Ratta Cheese Store, Sant' Agata dé Goti

Wheels of pecorino cheese, Antonio Della Ratta Cheese Store

Chapter 9
Holiday Dishes

Prima di Natale, no friddo e no fame,
dopo Natale, friddo e fame.
Before Christmas, no cold and no hunger,
after Christmas, cold and hunger.

Holidays marked festive occasions in the otherwise difficult life of farmers and shepherds in Southern Italy. Special foods were prepared on *il giorno d'onomastico,* the birthdate of the patron saint of the town, an ancient tradition preceding Christianity when the gods were honored with sacrifices on their special days. On feast days, townspeople in the contradas around Sant' Agata prepared holiday dinners in honor of their patron saints.

Each contrada had a different patron saint—Sant' Anna, San Pangrazio, Santa Flavia, and so on—and each saint was celebrated on a feast day. There were four or five feast days in the area, from the various contradas, and we went to all of them. They were all-day affairs. For San Michele, the patron saint of Contrada Capitone, they lit a big fire in the fields; they said it was because San Michele needed the light so he could see well enough to fill the *spiga,* the ears of wheat. Sometimes when the harvest was bad and the yield was small, they thought they did something wrong—maybe they didn't pray enough or they didn't light the fire up enough the past year—so on the feast day the following year they made extra sure the fire was big and bright and they prayed well into the night to San Michele for the blessing of a good harvest.

Being out in the country with not much entertainment, we couldn't wait as kids for the feasts to come. The biggest

was Sant Alfonso, in Sant' Agata in August, for all the contradas belonged to the commune of Sant' Agata. Our feast in the Contrada Sanqunito was the Madonna of Palmentata in May. While mothers and eldest daughters were cooking and setting up their homes for the feast, the rest of the family went to church, and the procession began after the mass. The *Processione della Madonna Palmentata* went through the various contradas, and the people cleaned and swept the streets, all the driveways, and they put flowers in the courtyards in her honor. The women along the way used to hang out hand-embroidered silk bed covers they had received from their mothers in their wedding *curredo,* trousseau; they hung them off their balconies like banners or on ropes across the front of their houses, with pictures of flowers in the middle of them, and the bride's initials. These coverings were used to decorate the beds on special occasions, like when they had special parties. The people picked rose petals, put them in a silver tray, and threw them to the Madonna as she stopped in the courtyards of the people's homes. She was carried by strong men; they put her down in the courtyard and the people threw *'a sciuriat,* rose petals, to her. Then they pinned money on her beautiful dress. Then they said a prayer, and she was picked up and carried along to the next contrada, a procession that took half a day, maybe ten miles. People who had received a prior miracle or

Blessing of the palms, Cefalu, Sicily, 1975 (right)

had been granted a wish by praying to the Madonna were especially eager to carry her, and they used to take turns to make sure everyone had the chance to carry her. We kids used to walk in the procession too. At the end of the procession, they brought the Madonna back to the church, which was decorated with beautiful flowers, and they left the church open all day for people to come and pray and ask for *il voto*, a special favor to cure the sick, or special favors for other wishes. Sometimes they brought gold and left it there, asking, *"Madonna mia, mammà sta malat, fatela sta bona!"* (My Madonna, my mother is not well, please heal her!) Then, after the prayers, the procession was over, and the Madonna was placed back on the altar, and they went home to eat their big *pranzo*. They had special dishes like *i fettucine all'uovo*, egg fettucine, capon, and rabbit, and for dessert, *anginettes*, cookies, and *i guanti*, fried dough tied into a knot and dusted with confectioners sugar. They made *pane pa Madonna*, a sweet bread with eggs and sugar. Then the men went to rest for a few hours while the women cleaned up.

By late afternoon, they freshened up, got dressed, and went to the *festa* just as it got dark. The husbands, wives, and children went back to the church to say a few more prayers and then went to the feast. A stage was set up in the middle of the field, next to the church of Palmentata, and hired singers came from Naples and other cities. Chairs were set up, but most of the people stood behind to listen to the music and to do *danze folcloristiche*, provincial folk dances.

The church families used to bring *doni*, offerings, in the form of cakes and desserts, and before the concert started, they put them on the stage and said, "This is my special *'dono alla Madonna,'*" my special gift to the Madonna and left a dessert. And the auctioneer, sometimes a girl, auctioned them to the crowd. The better the dessert and the better-looking the girl, the higher the bids. The money went to the church. They sold torrone, gelati, peanuts, hazelnuts, and roasted chestnuts. The concert started at nine o'clock and lasted until midnight. Then at midnight they had a beautiful fireworks display.

Pizzelle Cresciute
Fried Dough

My grandmother made three types of *pizzelle cresciute* at Christmas. One, for the children, was made with plain fried dough rolled in sugar. The second one was made with *alici*, anchovies. The third one was made with *baccalà*, salt cod, for Christmas Eve, as an hors d'oeuvre before dinner with a glass of wine. She made another with *i sciurill*, squash flowers, and another with cauliflower when in season.

SERVES 10 TO 12

PREPARATION TIME: 2 HOURS

7 cups sifted all-purpose flour

1 teaspoon salt

Pizzelle cresciute with baccalà

1 packet dry yeast

4¼ cups warm water

About 4 to 6 cups vegetable oil for frying

Granulated sugar, optional

In a large bowl, thoroughly mix the flour and salt. Make a well in the middle of the flour. Dissolve the yeast in 1 cup of the warm water, pour the yeast water into the well, and, using a wooden spoon, start bringing flour from the interior walls of the well into the middle. When the yeast mixture becomes a thick batter, gradually pour in the rest of the water, still bringing flour into the middle. When all of the flour is incorporated, beat the batter until smooth and shiny. Cover the batter and set aside in a warm place for 1 to 1½ hours until it doubles in size. Stir lightly.

Heat 1 inch of oil to 350 degrees in a large, deep skillet over medium heat, or use a deep-fryer set at 350 degrees. With a large spoon held in your writing hand, scoop out about ⅓ cup of the batter and, with your other hand, use a smaller spoon to slide the batter off the large spoon into the hot oil in one piece. Fry pizzelles in batches until they float and turn a nice gold color. Replenish oil if needed. Be aware that they cook very fast, in 1 to 2 minutes. Take them out with a skimmer and lay them out on paper towels to drain excess oil. Place them on a serving plate and serve hot or at room temperature. They can be served plain or rolled in granulated sugar.

Variations

Pizzelle Cresciute with Anchovies

Cut up 10 to 12 anchovies into ¼-inch pieces. Blend them well into the risen batter. Fry following the directions for plain *Pizzelle Cresciute*.

Pizzelle Cresciute with Cauliflower

Cut a cauliflower into small florets and blanch in boiling water for 5 minutes. Drain and cool. Stir the cauliflower into the batter. Fry following the directions for plain *Pizzelle Cresciute*.

Pizzelle Cresciute with Baccalà

Soak and poach a 10 to 12-ounce piece of *baccalà*, salt cod, as for Codfish Salad, page 64. Take it out of the water and let it cool. With a wooden spoon, break it into small pieces, add to the batter, and mix well. Fry following the directions for plain *Pizzelle Cresciute*.

Pizzelle Cresciute with Squash Flower

Wash 10 to 24 squash flowers well, patting them dry with a paper towel. Gently mix them into the batter so they don't break. Make sure when scooping out the batter that each pizzelle has a flower in it. Fry following the directions for plain *Pizzelle Cresciute*.

Pizzelle cresciute with squash flower

La siringa

Zéppole di Natale
Christmas Zéppole

SERVES 1 BIG FAMILY

PREPARATION TIME: 2 HOURS

1½ cups water

3 tablespoons butter

¾ cup dry white wine

¼ teaspoon salt

4 cups sifted all-purpose flour

4 large eggs

6 large egg yolks

About 4 cups vegetable oil for frying

2 cups sugar

Combine the water, butter, white wine, and salt in a medium-sized pot over medium heat and bring to the first bubble of a simmer. Remove from the heat, add the flour and, using a wooden spoon, mix vigorously until the dough forms a ball and detaches from the side of the pot, 1 to 2 minutes.

*Silvio and Claudio Georgio Suppa at the
Strega Factory in Benevento*

Transfer the hot dough to a marble slab or wooden board. With your fists or a rolling pin, repeatedly pound the dough down and gather it back up for 8 to 10 minutes, or until the dough is cool.

Put the dough in a mixer, preferably fitted with a paddle. Mixing at medium speed, add the whole eggs one at a time, waiting for each to be absorbed before adding the next, then add the yolks one at a time as well. When all the eggs are in and the dough looks smooth and shiny, turn the machine off and let the dough rest for 1½ hours.

60

Transfer the dough to a pastry bag fitted with a 1-inch star tip. (If you are lucky enough to have an old fashioned *siringa,* which is especially made for *zéppoles,* fit the metal tube with a disk that will form the shape you wish and roll the dough into long shapes that will fit into the tube.

In either a deep-fryer or a large, deep skillet or pot over medium heat, heat 1 inch of oil to 325 degrees. Squeeze 3- to 5-inch lengths of dough directly into the hot oil, making rings, straight lengths, or *S*-shapes. Fry slowly, turning once, until they are crispy and puffy and light brown. Be sure they are cooked through, not soggy in the middle. Replenish oil if needed. Remove them with a skimmer, place them on paper towels to absorb the excess oil, then roll both sides in sugar. Display them on a nice large platter and serve either hot or at room temperature.

On our trip to the Strega factory in Benevento, we were led on a tour by Pia dePalma, who encouraged us to include any of her famous company's recipes for the holidays.

Budino della Strega
Strega Pudding

SERVES 6
PREPARATION TIME: 30 MINUTES

3 large eggs

2 cups milk

⅓ cup sugar

Zest of 1 lemon, removed with a vegetable peeler

2 tablespoons unsweetened cocoa powder

⅓ cup Liquore Strega

Semisweet chocolate

Mix all ingredients except chocolate in a heatproof bowl or the top container of a double boiler. Place over gently simmering water and stir constantly until it thickens enough to coat the spoon. Do not heat the custard beyond 175 degrees or it will curdle. Discard the zest. Let the custard cool, then pour into fancy ice cream glasses. Shave some chocolate over each one, place in the refrigerator, and serve cold.

Vintage Strega bottles

Everyone got together in the house around *Carnevale,* Mardis Gras, during Lent and played a game *'Zi Nduniella,* old lady. In one room, young women dressed up as old women, along with the real 'Zi Nduniella. Sometimes women painted their faces with charcoal, or they covered themselves up with *'o maccatur,* a scarf, or an old dress, stockings, and a cane. When the game began, the man running the game let one woman at a time into the next room and the men lined up to guess if she was the real 'Zi Nduniella or not. When the dressed-up person came into the room, he asked, *"E chist è 'Zi Nduniella o no?"* If you guessed wrong, they'd hit you four or five times with *'o torciatura,* a sheet full of knots, and put you against the wall on your knees, and you were out of the game. If you guessed right, you made a guess about the next person. The young man who won would get a little prize and could choose the best-looking girl in the group to dance with, to a tune played by an old musician with an accordion. The young man also got to eat the special dessert of the house which was given to him by the girl he chose.

Pizza Rustica

Spaghetti Pie

SERVES 4

PREPARATION TIME: 25 MINUTES

3 large eggs, lightly beaten

⅔ cup grated parmigiano cheese

⅓ cup heavy cream

1 tablespoon chopped fresh Italian parsley

Salt and freshly ground black pepper

12 ounces cooked spaghetti, cold

2 tablespoons butter

About ½ cup plain dry bread crumbs

In a bowl, beat the eggs, cheese, cream, parsley, and salt and pepper to taste until well combined. Stir in the spaghetti, then set aside. Place the butter in a nonstick baking pan or a deep pie tin, melt the butter in a 450 degree oven, and spread over the pan bottom. Pour the spaghetti mixture into the buttered pan, spread evenly, and sprinkle lightly with bread crumbs for color. Bake at 450 degrees for approximately 8 to

Pizza rustica

10 minutes, or until it is firm and golden. Cut into as many pieces as you like. Serve hot or refrigerate and serve cold over the next few days. Either way is delicious!

Gamberi Vongole della Vigilia di Natale

Christmas Eve Shrimp and Clams

SERVES 4

PREPARATION TIME: 15 MINUTES

1 pound jumbo shrimp, shelled (2 to 3 shrimp per serving)

½ cup all-puprose flour

¼ cup extra virgin olive oil

6 cloves garlic, finely minced

½ cup dry white wine

½ cup chopped fresh Italian parsley

1 pound Manila clams or smallest available littleneck clams (4 to 5 clams per serving)

One 10-ounce bottle clam juice

2 plum tomatoes, chopped, optional

Salt and freshly ground black pepper

Dredge shrimp in flour, then shake off excess. Heat oil in a large skillet over high heat. Add shrimp and sear on both sides until lightly browned. Add garlic and cook, stirring frequently, until golden. Add wine and half of the parsley. Bring to a boil and cook until the wine is reduced by half. Add the clams, clam juice, tomatoes (if desired), and salt and pepper to taste, and bring to a boil. Cover and cook until clams are opened. Serve immediately over thin spaghetti or in bowls with lots of crusty hard bread to sop up the broth. Sprinkle with the rest of the parsley.

Vineyard on the Amalfi coast

Baccalà Anzalata
Codfish Salad

There was a boy, Luigi, who lived nearby us. They nicknamed him "Luigi Imbiccica" because he always mixed everything up and caused a lot of confusion in whatever he did. Around Christmastime his mother sent him across the fields to the *bottega*, the country store. His mother said, "*Luigi, va a accàtta nu chil 'i baccalà*" (Luigi, go buy me a kilo of codfish.) 'Zi Ndunetta was the *bottegara*, the store owner, and it was a general store where they sold a little bit of everything. She noticed Luigi in the store looking around as if he were lost. So she said to him, "*Luigi, che ti serve?*" (Luigi, what do you want?) He said, "*Ma 'Zi Ndunetta, maggiu scurdat che pesce voleva mammà*" (Aunt Antonette, I can't remember what kind of fish my mother sent me to buy.) Ndunetta said to him, "*Ma Luigi, si proprio nu baccalà!*" (But Luigi you are such a *baccalà*!) And Luigi's face suddenly lit up and he said to her, "*Ma 'Zi Ndunetta è proprio chella che vo' mammà, comm 'o sai tu?*" (But Aunt Antonette, how did you know? That's exactly the kind of fish my mom wanted!)

SERVES 4 TO 6
PREPARATION TIME: 2 DAYS FOR SOAKING, THEN 30 MINUTES

2 pounds dry *baccalà* (salt cod)

½ cup extra virgin olive oil

6 cloves garlic, coarsely chopped

½ cup fresh chopped Italian parsley

1 cup pitted Calamata olives

2 or 3 diced pickled hot cherry peppers, optional

1 lemon, cut into wedges

Soak the dry *baccalà* in abundant water for 2 days, changing the water twice a day. Cut into 3- to 4-inch squares. Layer the *baccalà* in a large shallow pot and add enough water to cover fish. Place over medium heat and bring to a simmer. Simmer gently for 10 to 15 minutes, or until the fish flakes when pressed with a spoon or fork. Remove from the heat and let cool in the cooking water to warm. With a skimmer, take out the *baccalà* and place on a large fish platter. Drizzle the fish with oil and sprinkle with garlic, parsley, olives, and cherry peppers if you like it spicy. Toss delicately so the fish breaks apart in large pieces. Garnish with a few additional parsley sprigs and lemon wedges. This dish can be served warm or cold out of the refrigerator over the next few days.

Baccalà Fritt
Fried Salt Codfish

SERVES 4 TO 6
PREPARATION TIME: 2 DAYS FOR SOAKING, THEN 25 MINUTES

2 pounds dry *baccalà* (salt cod)

2 cups all-purpose flour

4 cups vegetable oil for frying

Freshly ground black pepper

Fresh Italian parsley sprigs

1 lemon, cut into wedges

Soak the dry *baccalà* in abundant water for 2 days, changing the water twice a day. Cut into 3-inch square pieces. Roll the *baccalà* in the flour and shake off the excess. In a large, heavy frying pan, heat 1 inch of the oil until shimmery over medium heat. Carefully lay a single layer of fish in the pan and fry on both sides until light brown and crispy, adjusting the heat as necessary. Transfer to a fish platter and fry remaining fish, adding more oil to the pan if needed. Sprinkle with pepper to taste and garnish with parsley sprigs and lemon wedges. This dish can be served hot or cold out of the refrigerator over the next few days.

A Pizza e Ricotta
Ricotta Pie

This dessert was prepared around Eastertime. The recipe originates from my grandmother because she had a lot of cows that produced a lot of milk, and so she made ricotta cheese. She passed this recipe on to her daughters. She used to pour the milk into a big *caurar e rame*, a copper pot, and then put in *'o quaglio*, a small sack from the stomach of a baby lamb. Inside was rennet, a gel like heavy, fatty cream, that turned solid when it was hung to dry, like a sack of butter. She broke this sack into pieces and put it into the milk in the pot, covered it, and let it stay overnight.

The next morning the milk wasn't liquid anymore but had jelled like white gelatin—*quagliata,* as we used to say. Then she got all her wicker baskets, small and large, laid them on the draining board and, with her hands, scooped this *quagliata* into all the baskets. When the baskets were filled, she pressed down on the contents so that the curd separated and liquid, the whey, drained out through the basket for a few hours—the solid that remained was fresh basket cheese. It could be eaten fresh or used in desserts, pies, or any recipe. Whatever was leftover, she processed for dry cheese. Every morning for about two weeks, she left the cheeses by an open window where there was a draft. Then she laid a linen towel on the table, flipped the baskets upside down on the towel, salted the cheeses a bit, and then put them back into the baskets. She did this every morning for about two weeks, to dry out the cheese evenly on both sides. After two weeks, the cheese became firm and dry on the outside. At that point she removed the cheeses from the baskets and laid the wheels of cheese flat on tables covered with clean linen by the windows, where there was a draft that made the cheese dry faster. As the cheese went through the drying stages, from fresh to hard cheese, it was used for different things. Soft cheese was used in antipasti and sandwiches. At the end of the two-month process, the cheese became hard, and with a *rattacas,* a cheese grater, we grated it for our pasta dishes. After the cheese was dry enough, she used to rub it with oil and wrap it in *carta velina,* thin paper sheets, to stop the cheese from getting drier. This aged and preserved the cheese for months, and she stored the wheels away in a dry, cool place.

After she processed the cheese, she added some milk to the leftover whey and made ricotta. She simmered it slowly in the *caurar* over a low fire, stirring it constantly with a wooden spoon. After a few minutes, a white layer formed on the top of the liquid, which was the ricotta. She took a skimmer, skimmed the ricotta off the top, and laid it in a large basket lined with layers of cheesecloth. We never wasted *'o siel,* the leftover liquid, which she fed to the pigs with cornmeal, like a polenta. The pigs really enjoyed it and got fat from it. My grandmother followed the same process for goat cheese and pecorino cheese, named after the word *pecora,* sheep.

Scala on the Amalfi coast

SERVES 12 TO 14 (2 PIES)

PREPARATION TIME: 70 MINUTES

3½ pounds ricotta cheese, preferably fresh

3 cups half-and-half

2 cups sugar

10 large eggs

⅓ cup flour

2 teaspoons vanilla extract

2 tablespoons butter, softened (to grease the pans)

1 cup graham cracker crumbs

½ cup confectioners' sugar

Preheat oven to 425 degrees. In a large bowl, combine the first six ingredients and beat with a mixer at medium speed for 3 to 4 minutes, or until the batter becomes smooth. Grease 2 deep-dish pie pans or other shallow 2-quart baking dishes with butter. Sprinkle the graham cracker crumbs into the pans, tilt in all directions to coat, and lightly press the crumbs with your fingers to make them adhere. Pour the cheese batter into the pans, filling each pan three-quarters full. Bake at 425 degrees for approximately 50 minutes, or until the pies are firm to the center and golden brown. Let them cool completely. For a nice presentation, sprinkle the top with confectioners' sugar and rainbow shots and enjoy.

Babà al Rum

Rum Babas

This cake is traditionally eaten at Easter.

SERVES 12 TO 15

PREPARATION TIME: ABOUT 3 HOURS

Ingredients for the Cakes

1 cup whole milk

1 packet dry yeast

6 large eggs

½ cup sugar

1 pinch salt

4 tablespoons butter, melted and cooled

2½ cups all-purpose flour

12 metal baba forms, buttered and floured (or use a standard muffin tin or twelve 3-ounce ramekins, or a Bundt pan for one large cake)

Ingredients for the Syrup

2 cups water

¾ to 1 cup sugar

About ¼ cup dark Rum

Making the Cakes

In a small pan over low heat, warm the milk to lukewarm, remove from the heat, add the yeast, and mix until the yeast is completely dissolved. Pour the mixture into a large mixing bowl, then add the eggs, sugar, salt, and butter. Mix with an electric mixer fitted with a dough hook at low speed until well blended, then gradually add the flour. When the dough turns into a ball, increase the speed to medium and beat until smooth. The consistency should be like soft bread dough. With a spoon or your hand, scoop up enough dough to fill the prepared forms halfway. When all the dough is in the forms, place them on a baking sheet, put them in warm spot, and let the dough rise until the forms look full, about 1 hour. Bake in a preheated oven at 375 degrees for approximately 20 minutes, or until the tops are light brown and mushroom-shaped. While the babas are still warm, pull them out of their forms. Let them cool and then store them in a covered container at room temperature.

Making the Syrup

The next day, or even after several days (they last a long time), make some simple syrup by boiling water and sugar (adjust sugar depending on how sweet you want it) for 3 minutes, or until the sugar is dissolved. Cool the syrup to lukewarm and add rum to taste (¼ cup is good to begin with—you can increase it if you want it stronger). Arrange the babas on a rimmed baking sheet or dish, gradually pour the warm syrup over them, and let soak in the syrup, basting frequently, until they are nice and soft, about ½ hour. After soaking them, transfer them to a tray or plate, cover with plastic wrap, and refrigerate. Serve them cold or at room temperature. You can splash them with more rum when serving them, if you like, and they are also good with whipped cream.

Join we today.

It's American to disagree. It's also American to come together in the face of a challenge. And few challenges are as urgent as global climate change. More than a million people from all walks of life have come together to demand solutions. Now we need you. Take a minute and join us at wecansolveit.org. Together we can solve the climate crisis.

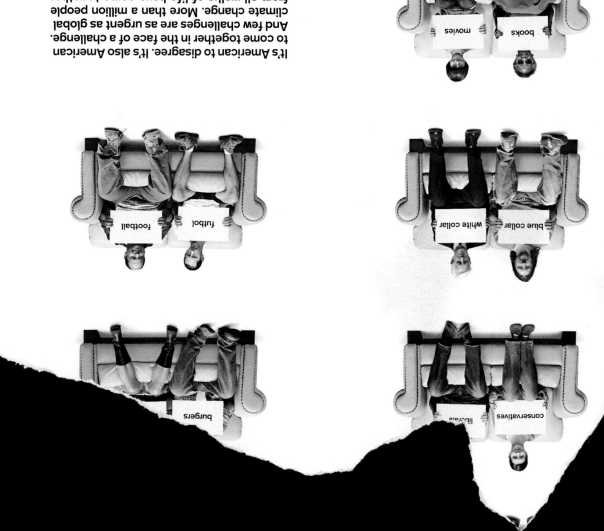

Rethink big.

THE SATURN OUTLOOK.™ THE EPA-EST. 24 MPG HWY, 8-PASSENGER CROSSOVER. WE'VE RETHOUGHT THE CROSSOVER BY MAKING ONE THAT GETS THE BEST FUEL ECONOMY OF ANY 8-PASSENGER CROSSOVER.[1] THE SPACIOUS THIRD ROW PROVIDES PLENTY OF ROOM FOR EVERYONE AND THEIR STUFF, MAKING SURE NOTHING IS EVER LEFT BEHIND. ADD ONSTAR.[®2] AND THERE'S NOTHING YOUR TROOP CAN'T DO. IT'S THE CROSSOVER FROM THE COMPANY THAT'S RETHINKING EVERYTHING. AS SHOWN $33,745. **STARTING AT $28,995.**[3]

24 EPA-est mpg hwy

saturn.com

1. Based on 2008 GM Mid SUV-Crossover segment and EPA-est. 16 mpg city, 24 mpg hwy. Excludes other GM vehicles. 2. Includes one-year Safe & Sound Plan. Call 1-888-4ONSTAR (1-888-466-7827) or visit onstar.com for details and system limitations. 3. Prices based on MSRP. Tax, title, license, retailer fees and optional equipment extra. Each retailer sets its own price.

John Dory Fish with "fingerprint" (St. Peter's Fish)

Pesce San Pietro Fritto Con Salsa di Peperoni Arrostiti

Seared John Dory Fish with Roasted Pepper Sauce

According to a legend still told to young children, meat should never be eaten on Fridays, especially on Holy Friday, when it would be considered blasphemy. Oral tradition in Sant' Agata tells the story of how Saint Peter, being a fisherman, didn't sell any fish on a particular day. When Jesus came by, Peter picked up a fish (legend has it that it was the John Dory fish, sometimes also known as St. Peter's fish) and showed it to Jesus, saying, *"Signore Jesu, nessuno si mangia pesce qua, cosa facciamo?"* (Signore Jesus, no one is buying my fish today, what shall we do?) And Jesus answered, *"Da oggi in poi, nessuna mangia piu carne, ma mangeranno pesce ogni Venerdi"* (From this day on, no one will eat meat on Fridays, everyone will eat only fish.) Peter left

his fingerprints on both sides of the Saint Peter's fish when he showed it to Jesus, fingerprints that can still be seen today if you look carefully. And this is why, according to local legend, people eat only fish on Fridays.

SERVES 4

PREPARATION TIME: 30 MINUTES

For the sauce

2 tablespoons olive oil

4 tablespoons butter

½ small onion, coarsely chopped

2 teaspoons minced peeled fresh ginger

3 large red peppers, roasted, peeled, and stems and seeds removed (or same amount of canned roasted red peppers)

½ cup dry white wine

¾ cup heavy cream

Salt and freshly ground black pepper

For the fish

⅓ cup olive oil

2 whole John Dory fish, 3 to 4 pounds each,
  filleted, or 4 filets 6 to 8 ounces each

1 cup all-purpose flour

2 cups steamed spinach, drained and kept hot

Making the sauce

In a small saucepan over medium heat, heat the oil and butter. Add the onion and ginger and sauté, stirring frequently, until the onions get soft and blond in color, 5 to 10 minutes. Add red peppers and white wine and cook for approximately 5 minutes, stirring a few times. Add cream and salt and pepper to taste. Let boil for 1 minute. Transfer the mixture to a blender and puree. Pour back into the saucepan and place on low heat to keep hot.

Cooking the fish

Heat the oil until fragrant in a large frying pan over high heat. Flour both sides of the 4 fish filets and place them in the hot pan, skin down. When the skin gets crispy and light brown, turn fish over. Turn heat to medium and cook the fish until firm. This should not take more than 5 minutes.

Ladle some of the sauce into the center of a large serving platter. Make a bed of steamed spinach over the sauce. With a slotted spatula, carefully remove the fish from the pan and arrange each filet on the spinach, using your own creativity. With a ladle, drizzle the rest of the sauce over the fish and some on the edge of the platter for a nice presentation.

Pesce e Spada Mediterraneo
Mediterranean Style Swordfish

SERVES 2

PREPARATION TIME: 25 MINUTES

⅓ cup extra virgin olive oil

Two 10-ounce swordfish steaks, approximately 1-inch
  thick

½ cup all-purpose flour

4 cloves garlic, finely chopped

⅓ cup dry white wine

12 to 15 ripe cherry tomatoes, cut in half

10 to 12 pitted Calamata olives

1 pinch dried oregano

1 teaspoon capers

1 cup fresh basil leaves, torn

Salt and freshly ground black pepper

About 1 cup fish stock or water

In a large frying pan, heat ¼ cup of oil over high heat until fragrant. When the oil is hot, flour both sides of the fish and place in the hot oil. Sear both sides until golden. Lower the heat to medium, add the garlic, white wine, cherry tomatoes, olives, oregano, capers, half of the basil, and some salt and pepper. Let cook for 2 to 3 minutes, stir the sauce ingredients, and add enough fish stock or water to almost cover the fish. Cover and let simmer for 5 to 8 minutes, or until fish is firm. Taste and adjust salt and pepper. Serve over pasta, pouring the sauce over the top, or with crusty peasant bread, drizzling with remaining olive oil and garnishing with remaining basil.

Taurasi landscape, Campania countryside

Chapter 10
Making Bread with 'a Nonna

Na cena senza pan è comm a na barca senza timone.

A dinner without bread is like a boat without a rudder.

My grandmother had three pieces of handmade wooden furniture in her kitchen besides the heavy dinner table that comfortably sat sixteen people and the heavy caned oakwood chairs. One was *'a fezzator*, which was a rectangular wooden tub with handles on either side. She used it to mix and store bread dough. The second was her *matarc*, a specially shaped tub that had four legs and a cover. The other piece was *'a cristalliera*, which was built into the wall. It had glass doors on top and drawers and cabinets with doors on the bottom, and it was where she kept all her glasswear, tablecloths, and china.

Her *matarc* was made out of a specially selected smooth wood by a particular *artigiano*, a fine craftsman, known as *'o falegname*, a highly skilled carpenter, who designed it for women who made a lot of homemade bread. It was perfectly smooth and could withstand any scraping without wear. At that time we had no refrigerators, and she used it to store loaves of bread and leftover food to be saved for later. My grandmother often caught me checking out what was in there to eat, and she used to say, *"Tu tieni semp' 'a cap inda matarc"* (You always have your head in the *matarc*).

When she made her bread, she put the flour into *'a fezzator* and formed the flour into a well shape, poured her dissolved homemade dried yeast and some water in the middle of it, and mixed it all together until she got the consistency she wanted. She dissolved the yeast in lukewarm water in a separate bowl. When the dough was mixed and kneaded, she took a ball of it, weighing about a pound, put it in a dish, covered it, and stored it at room temperature, where it began to ferment. Over the days, it dried out, and she used it as leavening in other baking. After that she began kneading the remaining dough, spreading it out in *'a fezzator,* then folding it over back to the middle, then kneading it again, for at least a half hour, until the dough was elastic and firm without any lumps. She rolled the dough into

Aunt Maria Morrone Capraro's oven, Sippiciano, 1973

a big ball for the last time, and then she picked it up out of the container and sprinkled flour on the bottom and the sides, so the dough wouldn't stick to 'a fezzator. Then she covered it and let it rise in a warm part of the kitchen. The next morning the dough had risen, doubling in volume, and 'a fezzator was full. She always knew exactly how much dough she needed to end up with a full fezzator.

In the morning she kneaded it down one more time, to get the air out, because it was all puffy and airy. Then she got the twelve cufanell, the wicker baskets, lined each one with linen cloth, sprinkled them with flour, and cut the dough into twelve pieces or whatever number of paniell, loaves of bread, she wanted to make that day. Then she rolled them into balls and put each one into a basket, sprinkling each one with flour so that they wouldn't stick to the linen cloth. Then she covered them by folding the linen cloth over the dough.

Then she left them in the cufanell, in a warm place, to rise a second time. The bread took about five to six hours in the morning to rise. While they were rising, she lit a fire in the oven using i fascine i len, twigs they brought back from the mountains, mixed with i spini, pricker bushes. She let the fire burn until the oven was thoroughly heated. With 'o munnul, a homemade broom made from leafy green branches tied to the end of a pole, she moved the ashes to either side of the oven until the 'o furn, the oven, was nice and clean so the ashes wouldn't get on the bread. She positioned her 'a parmassol, her long paddle,

Francesco and Francesca Caracciolo baking bread, Alvignano, 1975

flat and right at the mouth of the oven, sprinkled flour on *'a parmassol*, uncovered the *cufanell*, flipped one loaf over onto the paddle, and carefully pulled the cloth off so the bread stayed nice and puffy.

She put the first one in the farthest part of the oven, working her way out until the oven was all filled with bread. As she put the loaves in the oven, she pulled back the paddle quickly, jolting it with perfect arm action so the loaves slid off easily into the hot oven, exactly where she wanted them. She spaced them apart perfectly, spreading them so that as they baked and expanded, they wouldn't stick together. Then she got fine ashes and mixed them with water which became like a light cement paste. After all the loaves were in the oven, she'd cover the opening with *'a buccator,* the oven cover, completely sealing its edges with this ash paste so that no heat could escape. In those days there were no such things as thermometers to gauge oven heat. But she knew how to check the heat. When the bricks along the inside edge of the oven's opening turned white, that meant it was time to put the loaves into the oven.

She shook the *buccator,* breaking the seal, which fell off easily, to check if the bread was cooked. She picked up the loaves of bread and weighed them in her hand, bouncing them to check how heavy they were. If they were still too heavy, she'd say *"No, ancora, è troppo pesante"* (No, still too heavy), and leave it longer until it was done. When they were cooked the way she wanted, they were *leggiera,* light, as she used to say, which meant they were done. She checked the color too—light brown. And with *'a parmassol* she took them out and put them on the table to cool, then stacked them in the *matarc*. While the oven was still hot, she started preparing for *'a cena,* supper. She baked a tray of eggplant scarpone, chicken, or rabbit with potatoes.

Grandmother's sponge biscuits

Pullastro chi' Patan Nfurnat
Baked Chicken and Potatoes

SERVES 6

PREPARATION TIME: 1 TO 1½ HOURS,
PLUS 2 HOURS TO MARINATE

1 roasting chicken, about 3 pounds, cut into serving pieces

3 pounds potatoes, peeled and cut into large wedges

6 ripe plum tomatoes

1 onion, coarsely chopped

¼ cup fresh oregano leaves, torn, or 1 teaspoon dried oregano

½ cup extra virgin olive oil

Salt and freshly ground black pepper

Cut the tomatoes in half and squeeze the seeds out, then chop or tear them coarsely. Put all of the ingredients into a roasting pan and mix well. Let marinate at room temperature for 2 hours. Preheat oven to 400 degrees. Cover with aluminum foil (my mother used grape leaves), and bake for 40 minutes. Reduce the heat to 350 degrees, remove cover, and cook for about 20 minutes longer, or until the chicken releases clear juices when pricked with a fork.

'E Nfrennul (Taralli) i Santu Sriest
New Year's Eve
Taralli of Saint Sylvester

Taralli are crunchy, ring-shaped biscuits that are sort of like Italian pretzels. They are a very common snack food in southern Italy. Instead of fennel you can flavor them with dried onion flakes, garlic, sesame seeds, poppy seeds, peperoncini (crushed dried hot red pepper flakes), ground black pepper, or just plain salt. Feel free to experiment!

SERVES ONE LARGE FAMILY; MAKES ABOUT 24 TARALLI

PREPARATION TIME: ½ DAY

1 packet dry yeast

1 cup warm water

3 cups all-purpose flour

½ teaspoon salt

1 large pinch freshly ground black pepper

1 heaping tablespoon fennel seeds

Combine the warm water and yeast in a small bowl and stir until the yeast is completely dissolved. Stir in enough of the flour to make a thick batter. Cover with cloth and set aside in warm spot for 30 to 45 minutes, or until the dough begins to rise. Form the remaining flour as a mound on a wooden kneading board (my grandmother used a *tavulill*, a wooden disk) and make a well in the center. Add the salt, pepper, and fennel seeds, then the raised batter. Using your hand, gradually mix the dry flour into the batter until the ingredients are completely blended into a rough dough. Sprinkle flour on your work surface so that the dough won't stick. Knead the dough vigorously until elastic and smooth, adding a little more flour or water as you knead if the dough either remains sticky or is too stiff to manipulate. Roll the dough into a ball and place in a floured bowl. Cover with a damp cloth and let rise in a warm place for 2 to 2½ hours, depending on the temperature of the room, or until it doubles in volume. Put the dough back on the floured kneading board and cut it into small pieces. Roll them into ropes with your hand, approximately 8 inches long and ½ inch thick (it helps to keep your hands lightly floured as well). Now join the ends of each rope into a ring, overlapping the ends 1 inch and pressing with your thumb to seal them. Arrange the biscuits on 2 floured baking sheets. Let rise in a warm spot until doubled, 1 to 2 hours. Bake them in a preheated oven at 375 degrees for approximately 1 hour, or until they are light brown and crispy to the center. For the next few days enjoy them as snacks or serve to guests with a glass of wine just like my father, Ilario, enjoyed them with our homemade wine.

Viscuott Spugnat ra Nonna
Grandmother's Panzanella

After she had baked bread, my grandmother, never wasting anything, dried her figs, apples, tomatoes, pumpkin seeds, and all sorts of nuts in the oven as it cooled. Then, overnight, in the remaining heat, she dried *i viscuott*, biscuits. These were made from long loaves baked together with the bread. The loaves were deeply scored so that, once baked, the individual biscuits broke off cleanly. Left in the oven overnight, they became brittle and crunchy and they looked like big *freselle*. She used them for what is known today as *panzanella* but in those days was known as *viscuott spugnat*. She briefly soaked the biscuits in water and then broke them into a big bowl. Then she added oregano, onions, olive oil, and tomatoes.

SERVES 4–6

PREPARATION TIME: 15 MINUTES

3 Old World *viscuott*, or 12 *freselle*, or 6 slices crusty peasant bread, stale or toasted

6 ripe San Marzano or other plum tomatoes, or 15 ripe cherry tomatoes

1 small bunch fresh basil

½ cup extra virgin olive oil

1 large pinch chopped fresh oregano, or 2 pinches dried oregano, to taste

Salt and freshly ground black pepper

1 small red onion, slivered, optional

Submerge the bread in cold water for approximately 5 seconds, then quickly lift out. Let sit for a couple of minutes on a plate, until the excess water runs out. The bread should be moistened but still crunchy. Break the bread into pieces into a large bowl. With your hands, squeeze and break apart each tomato over the bread. Tear 8 basil leaves into the bowl and add olive oil, oregano, and salt and pepper to taste. Onion is

Viscuott spugnat ra nonna

optional. Mix gently until all ingredients are blended, garnish with more basil, and serve.

Note: Viscuott is the Neapolitan word the Sant' Agatese used for *biscotti*, or hard bread biscuits. Ring-shaped and rectangular *freselle* and *taralli* are other common *biscotti* which can be peppery, seeded, or plain. *Biscotti* are widely known as after-dinner dessert cookies to complement espresso or cappuccino. The recipes in this cookbook refer to *viscuott*, or *biscotti*, the hard bread version and not the sweetened type. In Italian American communities, bakeries and grocers offer *freselle* and many forms of *biscotti*.

Freselle

Chapter II
Family Recipes
'Zi Irma and 'Zi Giuannina

I fatt' rà pigniat' i sap' sul' 'a cucchiar'.
Only the spoon knows what's going on inside the pot.

Carmela's role as family matriarch reflected the social status of farming women who managed large families whose survival depended on many hands working long hours on the farms. Carmela taught her seven daughters how to sew, weave, spin, and handle household tasks, and they often joined in the fieldwork by hoeing, weeding, and carrying produce in baskets on their heads from the fields. To guarantee family survival in the South, even the youngest hands were needed to work in the fields. Children of farming families seldom attended school beyond the second or third grade of the two-room schoolhouse of their *contrada*. In a *contadina* society, where the concept of meritocracy did not exist, the chance to learn writing skills and complete a formal education was usually reserved for the upper classes, whose children attended universities and earned professional degrees.

The first written cookbook in Italy, *De Re Coqiunare,* appeared in the fourth century. It featured the recipes of Apicius, a Roman gourmet chef who lived during the reign of Emperor Tiberius. During the Renaissance, Bartolomeo Scappi, *il cuoco segretto dei Papi,* the secret chef of the Popes, wrote *Opera dell'Arte del Cucinare* as an instruction book to teach proper cooking techniques to his apprentices. In homes of the peasantry, *l'arte della cucina,* the art of cooking, was seldom written down; instead, it was stored in generational memory, with recipes and traditional ways of preparing dishes transmitted through the oral tradition. Southern women were unheralded culinary masters of the kitchen, seasoned veterans from lifetimes of practice and invention who taught their daughters the accumulated secrets of great cooking. Carmela's daughters, Irma and Giuannina, learned these recipes from her, and carried on the tradition of preparing these Campanian dishes for their families.

During my visit to the home of Silvio's eighty-seven-year-old aunt, 'Zi Giuannina, she told me she was known and respected as the strongest farm worker among the seven girls in the family, weeding, hoeing, carrying wheat from the fields, and milking the cows. "The other ones couldn't keep up with me," she said with a grin.

Ravioli Fritt di A 'Zi Giuannina (Sant' Agata)
Aunt Joanna's Fried Ravioli

Ricotta *impastata* is drained ricotta. If it is not available, use regular ricotta, drained in cheesecloth or a fine strainer for 20 minutes.

MAKES ABOUT 10 LARGE RAVIOLI
PREPARATION TIME: 3 HOURS
The Filling (Imbottitura)

5 large eggs, beaten

34 ounces ricotta *impastata*

Grated zest of 1 lemon

'Zi Giuannina (right)

1 teaspoon vanilla extract

½ cup candied fruit, cut into fine dice

1⅓ cups sugar

Combine all ingredients together in a bowl and give it a good mix, then cover and place in the refrigerator.

The Dough (sfoglie)

8½ cups sifted all-purpose flour, plus ½ cup for the board

2 large eggs

⅔ cup sugar

About 3 cups whole milk, plus more as needed

Place flour on a kneading board or marble slab and make a well in the center. In a separate bowl, beat 2 eggs and sugar until well blended. Pour the mixture into the well, add some milk, and mix in the flour with your hand from the inner rim of the well. Keep adding milk while mixing. When all of the flour has been mixed in and a rough dough has formed, knead in additional milk, if needed, to make a firm but malleable dough. Keep kneading the dough until smooth. Cut the dough into 3 or 4 pieces and roll them into balls. Set aside. Sprinkle flour on the kneading board. One at a time, place a ball in the center and roll the dough into a thin sheet approximately ¹/₁₆-inch thick.

With a bowl 4 to 5 inches in diameter, stamp out individual rounds of dough. Remove the excess dough, leaving the rounds on the board. Spoon equal amounts of the stuffing into the center of each round. Fold each round over into a half-moon, and use a fork to seal the ravioli all around. Once they are folded and sealed, set them on a floured baking sheet so they won't stick to the surface.

Frying and Serving

About 4 cups vegetable oil

Confectioners' sugar

In a large, deep frying pan or deep-fryer, heat 1 inch of oil to 350 to 375 degrees. Fry the ravioli in the hot oil a few at a time, turning once, for 2 to 3 minutes, or until golden. Remove them using a skimmer, and put them on paper towels to drain. Repeat the process until finished. Arrange them on a large platter or tray and sprinkle them with confectioners' sugar and serve hot, warm, or cold.

Chiacchiere di Carnevale di 'Zi Giuannina

Aunt Joanna's Carnevale Chiacchiere

SERVES 20
PREPARATION TIME: 2 HOURS

The name of this recipe comes from the Italian word *chiacchiere,* to chat. After dinner was finished, people chatted over this dessert. In a time before processed foods and desserts, families used whatever was on hand to make simple sweets with ingredients from the farm that they could afford.

6½ cups sifted all-purpose flour, plus ½ cup for the board

2 large eggs

2 tablespoons butter, melted

½ cup granulated sugar

1 teaspoon vanilla extract

Grated zest of 1 lemon

About 2 cups whole milk, plus more as needed

About 4 cups vegetable oil for frying

Confectioners' sugar

Place flour on a kneading board or marble slab and make a well in the center. In a separate bowl, beat the eggs, melted butter, sugar, vanilla, and lemon zest until well blended. Pour the mixture into the well, add some milk, and mix in the flour with your hand from the inner rim of the well. Keep adding milk while mixing. When all of the flour has been mixed in and a rough dough has formed, knead in additional milk, if needed, to make a firm but malleable dough. Keep kneading the dough until smooth. Cut the dough into 3 or 4 pieces and roll into balls. Set aside. Sprinkle flour on the board. One at a time, place a ball in the center and roll the dough into a thin sheet approximately ¹/₁₆ inch thick.

Cut the sheet with a knife into different shapes and sizes like strips, squares, rounds, and so on. Use your imagination.

In a large, deep frying pan or deep-fryer, heat 1 inch of oil to 350 degress. Fry them in the hot oil a few at a time, turning once, for 1 to 2 minutes, or until golden. Remove them using a skimmer and put them on paper towels to drain. Repeat the process until finished. Lay them on a large platter or tray and sprinkle them with confectioners' sugar. Serve and chat! Can be served hot, warm, or at room temperature, preferably with a cordial, either Strega or limoncello.

Suppa family portrait, 'Zi Irma second from left

Puparuol 'Mbuttinat di' 'Zi Irma

Aunt Irma's Stuffed Peppers

SERVES 6 TO 8
PREPARATION TIME: 1½ HOURS

6 to 8 red and yellow bell peppers

4 cups Italian bread, soaked in water and squeezed thoroughly

1 cup dry bread crumbs

½ cup chopped fresh Italian parsley

½ cup fresh basil, torn

1 teaspoon dried oregano

2 teaspoons capers

2 heaping teaspoons chopped fresh garlic

½ cup grated parmigiano cheese

5 anchovy filets, finely chopped

15 pitted Calamata olives, halved

3 eggs

⅓ cup extra virgin olive oil, plus ⅓ cup more for baking

1 cup water

Preheat oven to 400 degrees. Cut the tops off the peppers, core them, and save the tops. Place all remaining ingredients except the oil for baking and the water in a large bowl and mix well with your hands. With either your hands or a spoon, fill each pepper with the stuffing. Put the tops back on and wedge them standing up in a baking pan. Drizzle the peppers with ⅓ cup of oil and 1 cup of water. Bake for 30 to 45 minutes, or until the edges of the peppers start to brown. Lower the heat to 350 degrees and bake for approximately 20 minutes longer, or until the peppers are tender and the stuffing is hot. They can be served plain or with tomato sauce and grated cheese.

Aceto

Homemade Vinegar

PREPARATION TIME: 1 MONTH

8 cups red wine (preferably homemade, but if not, any fruity red wine will do)

4 medium slices yeast-raised bread

Puparuol 'mbuttinat di' 'Zi Irma

Pour the wine into a large-mouth glass decanter or an earthenware crock with a spigot. Add the bread to the wine and cover well with a cheesecloth stretched over the top of the container. Store at room temperature for 25 to 30 days. At the end of the fermentation period, filter the contents through cheesecloth or a coffee filter into a fresh decanter. Leftover sediment, called the mother, 'a mamma, can be substituted for the bread and reused to make a new batch of stronger vinegar.

Enjoy your homemade natural vinegar!

Scarola e Fasul
Escarole and Bean Soup

SERVES 4 TO 6
PREPARATION TIME: 45 MINUTES

1 head coarsely chopped escarole, well washed

⅓ cup extra virgin olive oil, plus more for serving

5 cloves garlic, chopped

4 cups chicken broth

1 cup cooked or undrained canned white
    cannellini beans

Salt and freshly ground black pepper

Peperoncino (crushed dried hot red pepper), optional

Fill a 4-quart pot halfway with salted water and bring to a boil. Add the escarole and cook for 10 to 12 minutes, stirring occasionally until the escarole is cooked *al dente*. Drain and set aside.

In the same 4-quart pot, heat oil over medium heat. Add garlic and cook until golden. Stir in the escarole, chicken broth, and the cannellini beans. Bring to a boil, turn the heat down, and simmer for about 10 minutes, stirring occasionally. Add salt and pepper to your liking, and peperoncino if you like it hot. Drizzle some extra virgin olive oil over each dish, if you like, and serve with crusty peasant bread.

Pan Cuott
Cooked Bread

SERVES 4 TO 6
PREPARATION TIME: 1 HOUR

⅓ cup extra virgin olive oil

4 cloves chopped garlic

Pan cuott

3 ounces diced prosciutto, optional

4 large slices crusty peasant bread, toasted or stale, cut or broken into pieces

4 cups of escarole and bean soup

1¼ cups grated parmigiano cheese

1 teaspoon peperoncino (crushed dried hot red pepper)

Heat oil in a large, nonstick frying pan, over medium heat. Add garlic and prosciutto when oil is hot and cook until golden. Add the dry bread and stir with a wooden spoon until the bread absorbs most of the oil. Add the escarole and bean soup. Turn the heat to low. Stirring constantly to prevent sticking, cook until the bread absorbs all the juice and the mixture is soft and moist but not runny. Add ¾ cup of the cheese and the red pepper and mix well. Turn off the heat and, with a wooden spoon, spread the mixture on a plate (or small baking pan), mounding it slightly in the center. Sprinkle the remaining cheese over the top and let rest for 10 minutes. You can serve it immediately, or you can bake it as my grandmother did, which was my favorite, at 400 degrees for approximately 10 minutes, or until the top gets light brown and crispy. I recommend it this way!

Options: You can replace the hard bread with *freselle,* which can be found in any good Italian bakery. Or, if you are in the right bakery, you might find Italian *viscuott,* like the ones my grandmother used to bake.

I Friarielli con Pomodorini di Collina
Green Peppers and Cherry Tomatoes

SERVES 6 TO 8

PREPARATION TIME: ½ HOUR

⅓ cup extra virgin olive oil

5 cloves garlic, lightly smashed with your hand or a kitchen utensil, peel discarded

3 pounds baby green peppers, stems removed, or cubanelle peppers, as small as possible, stems removed, and cut in half

1 pound cherry tomatoes

1 cup fresh basil leaves, torn

Salt and freshly ground black pepper

Heat oil in a large frying pan over high heat. When oil is hot, add garlic and cook, stirring, until garlic is blond in color. Add green peppers, lower heat to medium, and cook, stirring for approximately 2 minutes. Add cherry tomatoes, half of the basil, and salt and pepper to taste. Let cook for approximately 5 minutes, or until the peppers become soft but still retain their shape. Serve on a large platter, sprinkled with the rest of the basil.

Other options: Add Calamata olives and peperoncino (crushed dried hot red pepper) to the recipe.

This is an excellent *contorno,* side dish.

Piselli con Ventresca e Ova
Peas with Bacon and Eggs

SERVES 4 TO 6

PREPARATION TIME: 30 MINUTES

3 tablespoons extra virgin oil

4 ounces Italian *pancetta* (bacon), julienned

1 medium onion, sliced thinly

3 tablespoons butter

20 ounces frozen or shelled fresh peas

½ cup chicken broth or water

Salt and freshly ground black pepper

4 large eggs, lightly beaten

Heat oil in a large pan over medium heat. When oil is hot, add the sliced pancetta and cook, stirring, until crispy, approximately 3 minutes. Add onions and butter, stirring frequently for another 5 minutes, or until onions become translucent and soft. Add peas, chicken broth or water, and salt and pepper to taste.

Stir well and cook for another 4 minutes until the peas are tender. Add eggs and stir continuously until eggs are firmly cooked. Turn off the heat and serve in a large bowl. Contents should be moist but not wet.

Optional: Sprinkle parmigiano cheese over everything before serving.

This is an excellent *contorno,* side dish.

'A Giambotta
Vegetable Medley

SERVES 8 TO 10
PREPARATION TIME: 2 HOURS

½ cup extra virgin olive oil

1 large onion, coarsely chopped

4 cloves garlic, chopped

1 pound russet potatoes, peeled and cut into cubes

4 celery stalks, cut crosswise into 1-inch pieces

3 bell peppers (1 green, 1 red, and 1 yellow, for color), seeded and cut into 1-inch strips

1 large eggplant (about 1¼ pounds), unpeeled and cut into 1-inch cubes

1 to 1½ cups shelled fresh fava beans

1 pound cherry tomatoes, slit and squeezed to expel seeds

Water or chicken broth, as needed

12 fresh basil leaves, coarsely chopped or torn

½ cup coarsely chopped fresh Italian parsley

Salt and freshly ground black pepper

Heat oil in a large pot over medium heat. When oil is hot, add onion and garlic and cook, stirring frequently, until onion turns translucent and shiny. Add potatoes, celery, peppers, eggplant, fava beans, tomatoes, and salt and pepper to taste. Cover and let simmer for approximately 20 minutes. Stir frequently and check to make sure the contents are always moist, adding water or chicken broth as needed. After 20 minutes, add basil and parsley and taste for salt and pepper. Cook a bit longer, until all vegetables are tender but still retain their shape. Let stand off heat for 10 minutes. Serve in a large bowl or two.

Optional: Sprinkle with parmigiano cheese and peperoncino (crushed dried hot red pepper) and garnish with basil. You can also add some sausage or pork, cut into pieces and added to the hot oil before the onions.

This dish is excellent as a *contorno,* side dish.

Peperonata
Roasted Peppers

SERVES 4 TO 6
PREPARATION TIME: 30 TO 40 MINUTES

6 large yellow and/or red bell peppers

⅓ cup extra virgin olive oil

4 large garlic cloves, cut into slivers

20 pitted Calamata olives

2 heaping teaspoons capers

½ cup chopped fresh Italian parsley

Salt and freshly ground black pepper

6 tablespoons fresh bread crumbs

Cook peppers on a grill or bake on a sheet pan at 450 degrees, turning frequently, until charred all around. Place them in a closed brown bag and let rest for ½ hour. Take peppers out, remove stems and seeds, and peel. Cut into 1-inch strips and place in a bowl. Add oil, garlic, olives, capers, half of the parsley, and salt and pepper to taste, and give a good mix. Place in a shallow baking pan, sprinkle with bread crumbs, and bake at 400 degrees for 10 minutes, or until the top turns light brown and a bit crusty. Using a metal spatula, transfer them to a serving dish and sprinkle with the rest of the parsley.

This dish can be served hot, warm, or at room temperature and is excellent as a *contorno,* side dish with sandwiches or as a salad or appetizer.

Chef Silvio's Mussels Siciliano

SERVES 2 AS A MAIN COURSE,
OR 4 AS AN APPETIZER
PREPARATION TIME: 15 MINUTES

2 pounds Prince Edward Island mussels, washed and debearded

¼ cup extra virgin olive oil

2 tablespoons minced garlic (6 to 8 cloves)

2 tablespoons butter

2 tablespoons minced pickled hot cherry peppers

½ cup dry white wine

One 10-ounce bottle clam juice

½ cup chopped fresh Italian parsley

Salt and freshly ground black pepper

Heat oil in a medium-sized pot over medium heat. When oil is hot, add garlic, butter, and hot peppers and sauté until soft. Add mussels and stir to coat with oil and garlic. Raise heat to high, pour in wine, and bring to a boil. Cover and cook for 2 minutes. Add clam juice, salt and pepper to taste, and half of the parsley, cover, and cook just until all mussels open. Ladle into bowls, sprinkle with remaining parsley, and serve with hot crusty bread.

Sciurill, Cucuzziell, e Tall chi Spaghetti
Spaghetti with Zucchini flowers, Baby Zucchini, and Shoots

This was my grandmother Carmela's specialty. When the *sciurill*, or zucchini flowers, were still green buds, my grandmother picked them and some of the green tender shoots, *'i tall*. A few weeks later, when the plants were blossoming, she used the flowers to make several dishes. She stuffed them with ricotta (page 39), made *pizzelles* by deep-frying them in batter (page 59), and cooked them in omelets.

SERVES 4 TO 6

PREPARATION TIME: 30 TO 45 MINUTES

2 pounds mixed zucchini flowers, buds, tender shoots, and finger-length baby zucchini

½ cup extra virgin olive oil, plus more for drizzling

2 to 3 ounces end or scrap cut of prosciutto, coarsely chopped

8 cloves garlic, cut into slivers

½ cup dry white wine

Salt and peperoncino (crushed dried hot red pepper)

About 4 cups chicken broth or water

1 pound imported Italian spaghetti

Grated parmigiano cheese for sprinkling

Remove stems from zucchini, wash, and drain in a colander. Heat oil in a large pot over medium heat. When oil is hot, add prosciutto and garlic and cook until garlic is golden. Add squash mix, white wine, and salt and peperoncino to taste.

Cover the pot and cook for about 5 minutes, stirring a couple of times. Add enough chicken broth or water to almost cover the contents. Put the cover back on and simmer for 5 to 10 minutes, or until vegetables are tender but still intact. Taste and adjust seasoning. Set aside. Cook spaghetti *al dente*, according to directions on package. Add the drained spaghetti to the greens and toss everything together. Serve immediately in a deep bowl, sprinkled with grated parmigiano cheese, drizzled with extra virgin olive oil, and with a hearty peasant bread on the side.

Optional: Substitute fresh pork for prosciutto.

Zabaglione di Mia Mamma
My Mother Maria Suppa's Zabaglione

My mother used to make this for us kids before we went to school. She used to say, *"Chist' ti rinforza 'o cervello"* (this will make you smart).

SERVES 6

PREPARATION TIME: 15 TO 20 MINUTES

5 large egg yolks

2 large eggs

¼ cup sugar

⅓ cup plus 1 tablespoon dry Marsala

2 tablespoons brandy

1 teaspoon vanilla extract

Ground cinnamon, optional

Bring 2 inches of water to a gentle simmer in the saucepan of a double boiler over medium heat. (If you don't have a double boiler, fit a metal bowl or a small pan over the top of a larger pot or pan, making sure that the bowl or pan is over, not in, the simmering water.) In the top container of the double boiler (or in the metal bowl or small pan), whisk the egg yolks, eggs, and sugar until thick and pale yellow, always whisking in the same direction. Gradually whisk in the Marsala, then the

The road to the ancient Samnite city of Saticula, Faggiano (right)

brandy and vanilla. Place over the gently simmering water and, always whisking in the same direction at a steady speed, heat until the mixture has increased several times in volume and becomes thick and fluffy, 5 to 10 minutes. Be careful not to overcook. The correct final temperature is 160 degrees on an instant-read thermometer. Remove from the simmering water and serve at once.

There are different ways to serve this dessert: in a tall glass, sprinkled with cinnamon, either warm or cold out of the refrigerator; another way is in a bowl over fresh berries, topped with whipped cream.

Cucuzielli a Scapece
Zucchini Scapece Style

SERVES 4 TO 6
PREPARATION TIME: 1 HOUR

6 medium-sized zucchini (about 8 to 10 ounces each)

1 to 2 cups vegetable oil for frying

¾ cup extra virgin olive oil

1 bunch fresh mint leaves (approximately 2 dozen)

4 cloves garlic, cut into slivers

¼ cup red wine vinegar, preferably homemade (page 80)

Salt and peperoncino (crushed dried hot red pepper) to taste

Wash the zucchini, trim the ends off, and dry with paper towels. Cut them crosswise into slices, between ¼- and ½-inch thick.

Heat 1 cup of the vegetable oil in a large skillet over medium heat until shimmery. Add a single layer of zucchini slices to the skillet and fry until golden and tender, turning once. Place on paper towels to drain. Fry remaining zucchini in batches in the same way, adding more oil to the pan if needed.

Arrange the zucchini in layers in a deep glass bowl, sprinkling each layer with olive oil, mint leaves, garlic, vinegar, and salt and peperoncino. Let stand at room temperature for about 2 hours. Serve at room temperature or refrigerate and serve cold. This dish can be refrigerated and served several days later.

This dish is excellent for making a variety of sandwiches or as a *contorno*, side dish.

Mamma's Marinara Sauce

SERVES 12 AS A PASTA DINNER
PREPARATION TIME: 25 MINUTES

5-6 lbs. plum tomatoes, or 3 large (35-ounce) cans imported peeled tomatoes, preferably San Marzano

½ cup extra virgin olive oil

8 cloves garlic, lightly smashed with your hand or a kitchen utensil, peel discarded

½ cup coarsely chopped fresh basil

2 pinches dried oregano

Salt and freshly ground black pepper

Break up tomatoes with your hand. Heat the oil in a large pot over medium heat, add garlic, and cook until golden. Add tomatoes, basil, oregano, and salt and pepper to taste and stir well with a wooden spoon. Bring to a boil, stirring, then turn down the heat and simmer for approximately 15 minutes. Give a final stir and taste for salt and pepper. This marinara can be used in many recipes—chicken, fish, meat, and vegetables—or with plain pasta for delicious pasta marinara.

Cousin Mario's Limoncello

MAKES ABOUT 3½ QUARTS

4½ cups pure grain alcohol

Zest of 8 medium-sized lemons, removed with a vegetable peeler

9 cups water

4 cups sugar

Pour the alcohol into a stainless steel or glass container. Add the lemon zests and cover with plastic wrap. Store at room temperature for 8 days. On the eighth day, combine the water and sugar in a pot, place over high heat, and boil for 2 minutes, or until the sugar is completely dissolved. Remove from the heat and cool to room temperature. Take the lemon zests out of the alcohol and discard them. Pour the alcohol into the sugar and water; stir well. Pour contents through a fine strainer into bottles and seal with screw caps or corks. Store in a dry, cool place for 30 days before drinking. Once you open a bottle, keep this delicious cordial in the freezer. Enjoy this after-dinner drink with your friends and family!

(left) Street in Sant' Agata de' Goti

Chapter 12

Recipes from Campania

Chef Francesco Spagnuolo and Chef Carlo Russo

During our visit to the Mastroberardino Winery's Morabianco Restaurant in the grape-growing hills of Avellino, we entered a relaxing sunlit dining room decorated in blue, lavender, and green pastels with large windows that offered panoramic views of the surrounding vineyards. We met the talented, young head chef Francesco Spagnuolo in the kitchen, where he articulated his passion for the art of cooking. Francesco spoke with reverence about preserving traditional Campanian dishes and his vow to keep old ways alive by using time-honored farm-to-table ingredients. He attributed his successful career to having first learned *"la scuola vecchia della cucina,"* the old school of Campanian peasant cooking.

Maiale Patate e Pupacchie

Pork, Potatoes, and Vinegar Peppers

This recipe from Chef Francesco Spagnuolo, a well balanced dish and perfect for winter months, originates in the Irpinian mountains around Benevento and Avellino. A glass of Aglianico wine is a perfect match with this dish.

SERVES 4

PREPARATION TIME: 45 MINUTES

2 pounds boneless pork loin

1 pound pickled vinegar peppers (sweet, hot, or mixed)

1 pound potatoes

½ cup vegetable oil

Salt and freshly ground black pepper

Cut the meat into 1½-inch cubes. Take stems and seeds out of the peppers and cut into strips. Peel and cut potatoes into thick wedges. Heat the oil in a large frying pan over high heat. Add meat, peppers, and potatoes and cook, stirring constantly until the contents are brown and crispy. Add salt and pepper to taste. Turn heat to low and cook for an additional 15 to 20 minutes, or until the pork is cooked through and the potatoes are tender.

Mallone (Rape e Patate)

Broccoli Rabe and Potatoes

Originating in the Irpinian mountains, this dish is low in protein and has almost no fat but is rich in fiber—and *saziante*, satisfying and filling. Because of its high fiber content, this dish is consumed once a week. A glass of Greco di Tufo is a perfect match with this dish.

SERVES 4

PREPARATION TIME: 40 MINUTES

2 pounds broccoli rabe, tough ends trimmed

2 pounds potatoes

⅓ cup extra virgin olive oil

4 whole garlic cloves, peeled

Chef Francesco Spagnuolo in his kitchen at the Morabianco Restaurant, Contrada Corpo di Cristo

Chef Carlo Russo in his kitchen, Taverna Saticula, Sant' Agata de' Goti

Salt and freshly ground black pepper

Peperoncino (crushed dried hot red pepper), optional

Cut the broccoli rabe into 3-inch pieces. Boil in salted water for about 10 minutes, or until tender but not soft. Drain, reserving some of the cooking water. In a separate pot, boil the potatoes with the skins on until tender. Drain, peel, and chop coarsely. Heat the oil in a large frying pan over medium heat. Add the garlic and cook until blond in color, then add rabe, potatoes, and salt, pepper, and optional peperoncino to your liking. Cook 2 minutes, stirring frequently and adding enough cooking water to keep the contents moist. Serve hot.

Patate e Zucchini alla Menta e Pecorino

Potato and Zucchini with Mint and Pecorino Cheese

This classic Irpinian dish tastes best between the middle of May and the end of summer, when the ingredients are all in season. As Chef Spagnuolo said of these simple foods, "It's a dish of simple ingredients but very rich and healthy at the same time, as natural as the earth can offer."

SERVES 4

PREPARATION TIME: 45 MINUTES

⅔ cup extra virgin olive oil

1 medium-sized onion, coarsely chopped

2 medium-sized potatoes, peeled and cut into wedges

2 zucchini, approximately 12 ounces each, halved lengthwise, then cut crosswise into 1-inch half-moon pieces

½ cup dry white wine

Salt and freshly ground black pepper

¼ cup chopped fresh mint

1 cup grated pecorino cheese (possibly Paesano, from the hills of Benevento)

Heat ⅓ cup of the oil in a medium sized pot over medium heat. Add the onions and cook for about 2 minutes, then add the potatoes and cook for approximately 5 minutes. Add 1 cup of wa-ter, cover, and cook until the potatoes are half tender. Add zucchini, mix well, splash with the wine, and cook for approximately 15 minutes, or until the potatoes and zucchini are completely tender. Add salt and pepper to your liking, plus the mint. If necessary, add enough water to make the contents saucy but not too dry. Let stand off the heat for about 5 minutes, then ladle the *zuppa* into 4 bowls. Sprinkle with plenty of grated pecorino and drizzle with the rest of the oil. Enjoy it nice and hot, with slices of crusty Italian bread. You can add peperoncino if you like it spicy.

Zuppa di Cicerchie e Cicoria

Chickpea and Dandelion Soup

This dish is still prepared in the hills of Benevento by old farmers. *Cicerchie* are wild chickpeas—if they're not available, substitute regular chickpeas.

SERVES 4

PREPARATION TIME: 2½ HOURS
(AFTER SOAKING BEANS OVERNIGHT)

8 ounces dried *cicerchie*, or chickpeas, or 20 ounces undrained canned

¾ cup extra virgin olive oil

4 whole garlic cloves, peeled

Salt and freshly ground black pepper

2 pounds dandelion greens, well washed

Peperoncino (crushed dried hot red pepper)

Soak the *cicerchie* overnight in abundant water. Drain, transfer to a pot, and add enough fresh water to cover by approximately two inches. Bring beans to a boil, skimming off any foam that develops, then reduce the heat so that the beans simmer gently. Cook until tender, approximately 2 hours. Drain, reserving 2 cups of the cooking water. Heat ¼ cup of the oil in the pot over medium heat, add 2 of the garlic cloves, and cook until the garlic is blond in color. Add the *cicerchie* and salt and pepper to taste and cook, stirring, for 5 minutes to bring out the flavor. Puree the contents in a blender or food processor, adding enough cooking water to puree consistency. Return to the pot and set aside.

While the beans are cooking, fill another pot with boiling salted water, add the dandelions, and cook for about 10 minutes, or until tender but not mushy. Drain and set aside. In a medium-sized frying pan, heat ¼ cup of additional oil over medium heat. Add the remaining 2 garlic cloves and cook until gold in color, then add the dandelions and salt, pepper, and peperoncini to taste. Cook, stirring, until the dandelions are hot and well coated with oil.

Reheat the puree to a simmer, pour it into a large deep bowl, and lay the dandelions in the center. Serve this dish nice and hot, drizzled with the rest of the oil.

Following the career footsteps of his restaurateur grandfather Paoluccio, Chef Carlo Russo received his culinary degree in 1959 and worked as a chef in Switzerland and northern Italy. He eventually returned to Sant' Agata de' Goti to continue operating the Taverna Saticula that his grandfather had started in 1927, named in honor of the ancient Samnite settlement nearby. Carlo's eyes sparkled and he became animated when talking about cooking traditional Campanian dishes that followed ancestral recipes he had recorded over the years. Considered a local gastronomic historian and expert of authentic Sant' Agatese cuisine, Chef Russo's menu featured dishes from recipes passed down through the centuries from Roman, Lombard, Byzantine, Norman, and Spanish Bourbon influences to the region.

Costollette di Cinghiale alla Mele Annurca

Boar Chops with Apples

Carlo Russo's Taverna Saticula in Sant' Agata was started by his grandfather in 1927. This recipe originated in the ducal kitchens of the Lombard court in Sant' Agata in the sixth century.

SERVES 4
PREPARATION TIME: 30 MINUTES

¼ cup extra virgin olive oil

Four 10-ounce wild boar chops or center cut pork chops

½ cup all-purpose flour

4 tablespoons butter

3 medium-sized apples, cored, peeled, and cut into ½-inch cubes

½ cup apple brandy

2 bay leaves

½ cup dry white wine

Salt and freshly ground black pepper

Heat the oil in a large frying pan over high heat. Lightly flour the chops and cook them in the hot oil, turning once, until done to your liking (we recommend medium). Place them on a large platter, cover, and set aside. Add the butter and apples to the hot pan, splash them with brandy, and add the bay leaves. Stir well and add the wine. Let the sauce reduce over high heat until it thickens and the apples are tender but still firm. Add salt and pepper to taste, pour the sauce and apples evenly over the chops, and serve.

Insalata del Duca Marino

Duke Marino's Salad

This salad originated with the Byzantines, who governed Sant' Agata under Duke Marino from 877 to 896. Despite being constantly at war to protect their conquered territory from contending Lombard and Arab invaders in southern Italy, the Byzantines were known to organize great hunting expeditions for wild game, which they consumed at their festive celebrations.

SERVES 4
PREPARATION TIME: 30 MINUTES

1 pound boneless beef chuck

1 small red onion, thinly sliced

4 hard-boiled eggs, each cut into 4 wedges

1 medium-sized zucchini, trimmed and thinly sliced

4 medium-sized tomatoes, cut into chunks

1 cup pitted Calamata olives

½ cup chopped fresh Italian parsley

About ¾ cup extra virgin olive oil

About ¼ cup apple cider vinegar

Salt and freshly ground black pepper

To expedite this recipe, you can cook and refrigerate the beef and eggs 1 day before assembling the salad.

Boil the beef in salted water to cover until tender, approximately 2 hours. Let cool and cut into 1-inch cubes. In a large bowl, combine the beef, onion, eggs, zucchini, tomatoes, olives, and half of the parsley. Dress the salad with oil and vinegar; add salt and pepper to taste. Give it a good stir with your hands, like my grandmother used to teach me, saying, *"Anzalat adda ess cunciat chi mani, accussi è chiu sapurit, a bella nonna"* (Salad always tastes better when it's tossed with the hands, grandma loves you.) Give it a final taste and adjust the oil, vinegar, salt, and pepper to your liking. Transfer to a nice serving bowl. Sprinkle with remaning parsley. Serve and enjoy.

Tagliatelle di Simpaticio
Simpaticio's Tagliatelle

This tagliatelle recipe was named after the Byzantine general Simpaticio, who defeated the Lombards and took control of Benevento and Sant' Agata de' Goti in 877.

SERVES 4

PREPARATION TIME: 45 MINUTES

¼ cup extra virgin olive oil

3 ounces bacon or salt pork, cut into small, thin strips

1 medium-sized onion, thinly sliced

4 cups dandelion greens, well washed and coarsely chopped

½ cup dry white wine

Salt and freshly ground black pepper

2 pounds fresh egg tagliatelle, or 1 pound dried

½ cup pignoli nuts

6 ounces fresh basket pecorino cheese or goat cheese, cut into ½-inch cubes

Combine the olive oil and bacon or salt pork in a large frying pan over medium heat. Cook until the bacon is crispy, stirring to keep it from sticking. Add the onions and cook until translucent. Add the dandelion greens and white wine, cover, and cook for approximately 5 minutes, or until the dandelions are tender. Add salt and pepper to taste, stir, put the cover back on, and set aside off the heat.

Bring a large pot of salted water to a boil over medium heat. For fresh pasta, boil until the tagliatelle rise to the top; for dry tagliatelle, follow directions on the package for *al dente*. Drain, reserving some of the cooking water. Add the tagliatelle to the

Chef Carlo Russo, Taverna Saticula

contents in the frying pan and return to medium heat. Add the pignoli nuts and cheese. Give it a good stir. If necessary, add enough pasta water to moisten it. Give a final taste and add salt and pepper if necessary. Using pasta tongs, transfer the tagliatelle to individual bowls. Spoon any loose ingredients and sauce in the pan over each bowl of tagliatelle. Serve immediately.

Chapter 13

La Raccolta

Nu pranz senza vin, è comm a 'na iúrnata senza sole.

A meal without wine is like a day without sun.

For farming families around Sant' Agata, the *raccolta*, the harvest at the end of the growing season, was the reward for a hard period of labor on farms from spring to fall. From July to October, when all the crops were harvested, we decided what we needed to live on through the rest of the year. So my grandfather *facev i conti*, that is, he figured out what the family needed to survive until the next *raccolta*. Then we sold the excess—wine, corn, wheat, oats, beans, olive oil, and tomatoes—through *'o sanzano*, a local broker. Each *contrada* had a broker who came around and set up contacts between the farmers and the buyers from wineries and bread and pasta factories who bought the crops *all ingrosso*, wholesale. On the local level, we sold to people from town—rabbits, chickens, and eggs. *I signori*, the well-to-do from town, came by horse and wagon or with a *Ballila*, a car from that era, to buy eggs, fruit, grain, and corn. Oftentimes the *pulliere*, the chicken man, stopped by on his bicycle to buy eggs and chickens, filling a large basket attached to the handlebars and delivering the goods to doctors, pharmacists, and lawyers who relied on the farm for survival. During the war years, even the wealthy were near starvation, and they often appeared at the door of our farm almost begging for something to eat. The money earned from the sale of crops during the *raccolta* was put aside for the children's marriage expenses. Some of the money went to the *pannazzaro*, a *venditore ambulante*, a street vendor, who came around once a week and sold linens for the *curredo*, the marriage dowry for *'a nonna*'s seven daughters. In the case of boys in the family, the money from the sale of crops went towards buying furniture and putting an addition on the father of the groom's house, where the son would come to live with his wife. It was the custom for the groom to provide housing and furniture to the bride.

When we started to process all the crops from the harvest for the winter, *'a nonna* made sure everything was clean. She often washed bottles over and over,

(left) Vineyard with poppies in Campania region

sometimes using sand to rid them of any impurites, and she scrubbed pots and pans thoroughly. She made sure aprons were always worn and the hair was always covered around the kitchen. During the harvest, we washed the tomatoes in big tubs. They were cut lengthwise, the seeds squeezed out, and then put in bottles. Then we put in salt and basil leaves and packed them in tightly, corked the bottles, and tied the tops so that no air got into the bottles. The corks were first put in boiling water to soften and expand them. They were bigger than the bottle openings, and it was hard work to get the swollen corks into those bottles. But my grandmother used to say, *"Silvio, 'fallo buono! Tu si forte, 'a nonna, capito!"* (Do it right, grandmother loves you, because you're strong, understand!)

Then, in a huge kettle in the fireplace, we put fifty filled bottles, covered them with water, and brought them to a boil for five minutes to sterilize them. Then we put them on the shelves. Next we picked all the basil, chopped some up with oil for basil pesto sauce, and put it in jars, and that's what we used in the winter. The garlic from the garden was hung to dry from the ceiling of the *granaio,* our food pantry. We put up our pickled peppers, olives, and fresh olive oil in great yellow clay *ziri* and *anfore,* which were shaped like amphorae, with two handles, just like the ones they used in the ancient world for transporting wine and olive oil. Olives, cherry peppers, and hot and sweet peppers were cleaned and the stems removed before being put into the amphorae. Then we added

Farm women on the Amalfi Coast, picking sarchiapone, large, long zucchini

some garlic cloves and herbs and filled the amphorae half with vinegar and half with water, and we put a brick on top. That kept them perfectly preserved in the *granaio* during the winter months. We never went shopping anywhere. All our shopping was from our *granaio*; all of our food came from our garden and the cured, dried meats from our farm animals—cows, pigs, chickens—was there. At the end of the *raccolta* came *la vedemmia*, winemaking season, and we picked and carried all the grapes to the house. I remember them mashing the grapes with their feet and later as the years went by, with a machine. Then we put the grape juice, *'o must*, in large wooden barrels and pressed the *vinaccia*, which was the stems, seeds, and skins of the grapes, and also added this juice to the barrels. Then we made grappa with the pressed *vinaccia*.

Grapes and wine played an important role in dishes prepared around the harvest. People used to say, *"Chill' affare, come è ghiut'?"* (That deal, how did it go?) And they'd answer, *"O fatto è ghiut' a fini 'a tarallucci e vino"*—it went just like taralli and wine, meaning a friendly deal ended well for everyone, and they'd sit down and have a drink of wine and eat some taralli to celebrate.

Petti di Pollo Veronica
Breasts of Chicken Veronica Style

SERVES 2 TO 4

PREPARATION TIME: 20 MINUTES

⅓ cup vegetable oil

4 boneless, skinless chicken breasts, 4 to 6 ounces each

½ cup all-purpose flour

4 tablespoons butter

2 teaspoons shallots, finely chopped

⅔ cup *'o must* (wine right from the press before fermenting) or *vino spumante* (sparkling wine)

1 cup seedless mixed white and red grapes

Salt and freshly ground black pepper

Water or chicken broth

Heat oil in a medium-sized frying pan over medium heat. Flour the chicken breasts on both sides and brown well in the hot oil, 2 to 3 minutes each side. Spoon most of the oil out of the pan, add the butter and shallots, and cook, stirring, until the shallots are golden. Add *'o must* or *spumante*, grapes, and salt and pepper to taste. Cook 2 to 3 minutes longer, making sure the chicken is thoroughly cooked. Add some water or chicken broth if there is not enough juice left in the pan to make a sauce. Arrange the chicken on a platter and cover with the grapes and sauce. Serve nice and hot and enjoy.

Filetto di Manzo al Vino Rosso
Filet Mignon Steaks with Red Wine

SERVES 2

PREPARATION TIME: 30 MINUTES

¼ cup vegetable oil

4 filet mignon or other beef tenderloin steaks, about 4 ounces each

½ cup all-purpose flour

4 tablespoons butter

2 tablespoons shallots, finely chopped

⅔ cup dry red wine

Salt and freshly ground black pepper

Heat oil in a medium-sized frying pan over high heat. Flour the steaks on the top and bottom but not the side. Sear the beef on both sides. Spoon most of the oil out of the pan, add the butter and shallots, and cook until the shallots are golden. Add the wine and salt and pepper to taste. When the steaks are cooked to your liking, transfer them to a plate. If necessary, boil the sauce for 2 or 3 more minutes, until it reduces and thickens. Pour the sauce over the steaks and serve immediately.

You can substitute New York strip steak or any other type of steak for the filet mignon. You can also cook some sliced portobello mushrooms with the steak and serve them as a *contorno*, a side dish.

Ingredients for Grandmother's egg fettucine

Chapter 14

Sunday Dishes on the Farm

Sunday was usually a day of rest for farming families in the *contrada*s. After feeding all the animals, Silvio's family dressed for Sunday Mass and made the one-mile trip by foot or horse-and-wagon.

One Sunday morning my grandfather asked my Uncle Ginesio to help him finish up some work in the fields, picking beans and bringing them back to the courtyard. So Uncle Ginesio said to my grandfather, *"Angelo, cuando Dio ha creato l'universo, e lavorò sei giorni e il settimo giorno, si riposò. Oggi é giorno festivo e non si lavora."* (Angelo, when God created the universe, he worked six days and on the seventh, he rested. Today is Sunday and you're not supposed to work.) My grandfather shot right back, *"Si, oggi é giorno festivo, non si lavora, e non si mangia!"* (Sure, today is a holiday, but if you don't work, you don't eat!)

On Saturday nights, *'a nonna* made *fettucine all'uovo*, noodles made of eggs and flour. She rolled the dough into a sheet, then cut the sheet into long, wide ribbons and hung them to dry. By Sunday morning, the pasta ribbons had dried to a leathery consistency and she cut them into *fettucine*. With *'a passione*, she made a purée of fresh tomatoes for her sauce. The secret of her tasty sauce was a *tianiella e creta*, a heavy clay pot. Unlike metal pans, which allow the heat from the fire to penetrate quickly, almost as though in direct contact with the flame, clay pots, because of their thickness, distribute the heat in the pot evenly to the food. She started her Sunday sauce, made with sausage, pork, and beef, at seven o'clock in the morning and cooked it slowly. She used onions instead of garlic for Sunday sauce and sautéed them with the meat. When the meat and onion carmelized, she added some red wine. Then she added the fresh tomato purée, covered the pot, and cooked it slowly. The family went to church at San Michele and when we returned, the whole house was filled with the aroma of sauce. We set the table for at least twenty people. She'd cook the *fettucine* and toss it with her sauce, adding her homemade *formaggio i vacca,* cow cheese. Then my grandfather would go into the *cantina,* the cellar, to get his homemade wine and it would be a big feast every Sunday for her nine children and all her grandchildren!

In the afternoon, I used to go out with my Uncle Ginesio, and we would take a rest under a great oak tree, next to the fig trees and vineyard. After, we went to *'a stalla,* the barn, to milk the cow. He would say to me, "Silvio, come over here and open your mouth," and then he'd squeeze the udder and squirt warm delicious milk into my mouth. Singing songs, he used to put me on his shoulders and walk out to the fields to pick fruits.

Fettucine della Nonna
My Grandmother's Egg Fettucine

SERVES 6 TO 8

PREPARATION TIME: ½ DAY TO MAKE AND DRY THE PASTA,
20 MINUTES TO COOK PASTA

6 to 7 cups all-purpose flour

8 large eggs

½ teaspoon salt

Water, if needed

Braciole with Chef Silvio's Sunday Sauce

Get out your *tavulill* (page 3) or find a smooth wood or marble surface to work on. Put 6 cups of flour in the center and, with your hands, shape the flour in the form of a well. Add eggs and salt into the well. Using your hands, start to bring the flour from the inner rim of the well into the center, blending it with eggs. Keep blending until all flour is gone and you can shape the dough into a ball. You may need to adjust the firmness of the dough, adding more flour if it's too soft and adding water if it's too hard. Knead the dough until it becomes smooth and elastic. Now we're ready to make *'a pettola,* which means to roll out the dough into sheets, either with a rolling pin or with a pasta machine. Divide the dough into manageable pieces and roll into sheets approximately 1/16-inch thick. Cut the sheets into long 6-inch-wide ribbons, then cut the ribbons crosswise into fettucine 1/4- to 1/2-inch wide according to your liking, either with a knife or with a pasta machine. Sprinkle some flour on the table and spread out all the fettucine. The pasta can be cooked immediately or the next day. Always make sure your sauce is ready before you cook the fettucine. Keep in mind that fresh fettucine cooks quickly. Cook the pasta in boiling salted water. As soon as it starts to float and the water returns to a boil, drain immediately and serve with your favorite sauce.

Chef Silvio's Sunday Sauce and Braciole

SERVES 12 TO 15
PREPARATION TIME: 2 TO 2½ HOURS

2 pounds flank steak for *braciole,* butterflied, pounded ¼-inch thick, and cut into 4 rectangles approximately 8 inches long and 4 inches wide

Salt and freshly ground black pepper

4 cloves garlic, sliced thinly

4 sprigs fresh Italian parsley

1 cup extra virgin olive oil

½ cup all-purpose flour

1 pound fresh Italian sausage, cut into 3-inch pieces

1 pound pork spare ribs or babyback, or beef short ribs, divided between the bones and cut into 3-inch pieces

1 medium-sized onion, finely chopped

¾ cup dry red wine

3 large (35-ounce) cans Italian tomatoes, put through a food mill to remove the skin and seeds

1 large (20-ounce) can tomato purée

Lay the 4 pieces of flank steak on a cutting board and sprinkle them with salt and pepper and garlic. Place a parsley sprig on each slice. Roll up each slice from a short side and tie with butcher twine to make the *braciole.*

Heat the oil in a large, heavy pot over high heat. Lightly flour the *braciole* and lay them in the hot oil. Add the sausage and ribs. Using a wooden spoon, keep turning the meats until they are brown and crispy all around. Add the onions and keep stirring until they are carmelized. Add the red wine and, still stirring, let bubble for about 2 minutes. Add the tomatoes and the purée and some salt and pepper. Stirring frequently, bring the sauce to a boil. Adjust the heat so the sauce simmers slowly, cover, and cook for 2 hours, stirring periodically and tasting for salt. Add salt a little at a time, until it's to your liking. Watch for consistency, especially toward the end of cooking—it may need some water if it gets too thick and threatens to scorch.

Cook your favorite pasta or My Grandmother's Egg Fettucine (page 100). Drain the pasta and toss in a bowl with some of the sauce. Top with more sauce and sprinkle with an abundance of grated parmigiano cheese. Place the fettucine in the middle of the table and the mixed meats in another bowl right next to it so that everyone can help themselves. If you prefer individual servings, divide the fettucine into as many servings as you need and top each one with more sauce, and sprinkle with cheese.

Chef Silvio's Sunday Sauce is available in supermarkets if you don't have time for this recipe.

Pummarola 'Mbuttinat

Stuffed Tomatoes

SERVES 6 TO 8
PREPARATION TIME: 1½ HOURS

6 to 8 large ripe tomatoes

5 cups cooked Arborio rice, cold

½ cup chopped fresh basil

½ cup chopped fresh Italian parsley

1 teaspoon dried oregano

2 teaspoons small capers

2 teaspoons garlic, finely chopped

½ cup grated parmigiano cheese

12 pitted Calamata olives, halved

3 large eggs

½ cup extra virgin olive oil

Salt and freshly ground black pepper

Preheat the oven to 375 degrees. One at a time, cut the tops off the tomatoes with a sharp paring knife, then cut all around the inside of the tomato and hollow it out with a spoon. Be careful not to break the walls of the tomatoes. Finely chop enough of the pulp to make 1 cup and save for the stuffing. Place all the tomatoes in a baking pan, reserving the tops.

Mix half of the oil, the pulp, and all remaining ingredients in a bowl. Add salt and pepper to taste. Stuff the tomatoes with this mixture using a spoon. Place them in a baking pan and put the tops back on them. Drizzle the rest of the oil over each one and add enough water to cover the bottom of the pan (to prevent burning). Bake at 375 degrees for 35 to 45 minutes, or until they start to sizzle and are brown around the edges. Be careful not to overcook them so that they don't split or collapse. Carefully slide a spatula underneath each one and transfer them to a serving platter. Spoon the oil and juice in the pan over each one. Sprinkle grated cheese and chopped parsley over the tops if you like. If you have leftover stuffing, freeze it in a covered container and use it for stuffing tomatoes, zucchini, or peppers.

Croquette di Patate
Potato Croquettes

MAKES ABOUT 25 CROQUETTES

PREPARATION TIME: 1 HOUR

2 pounds potatoes

4 tablespoons butter, softened

¾ cup heavy cream

Salt and freshly ground black pepper

8 large eggs

⅔ cup grated parmigiano cheese

1 cup shredded mozzarella cheese

½ cup chopped fresh Italian parsley

1½ to 2 cups all-purpose flour

2 to 3 cups dry bread crumbs

4 to 6 cups vegetable oil for frying

Peel the potatoes and boil them until they are soft. Drain and place in a bowl. Add butter, heavy cream, and salt and pepper to taste, and mash them well. Set aside until cooled. Add 3 eggs, parmigiano, mozzarella, and half of the parsley and mix well. Form the mixture into ¼-cup balls using your hands or an ice cream scoop. Beat the remaining eggs in a bowl. Place 1½ cups flour and 2 cups bread crumbs in two separate bowls. Roll each croquette in the flour, then the eggs, and finally the bread crumbs, replenishing the flour and/or crumbs, if necessary. When all of the balls are coated, shape each croquette into a 2- to 3-inch oblong by rolling it gently between your hands, shaping in the same order in which the croquettes were coated.

Pour enough oil into a large, deep frying pan or deep-fryer to make a depth of 1 inch, and heat the oil over medium heat to 350 degrees. Working in batches, carefully transfer the croquettes to the hot oil with a skimmer and fry for approximately 4 minutes, or until golden brown. Keep the oil temperature steady and add more oil to the pan if needed. As they are fried, transfer croquettes to paper towels to drain. Arrange them on a serving plate, sprinkle with the rest of the parsley, and serve hot.

Tianiella e creta

Chef Silvio in his kitchen at Café Allegre

Chapter 15
Olive Picking in the Hills

Tu si comm a l'uoglio, ti trovi sempe a copp.

You are like oil, you always want to be on top.

Silvio recalled traveling by oxen and wagon to the nearby hills of Palmentata where, with large burlap sacks over their shoulders, he picked olives alongside his grandfather Angelo, Uncle Ginesio, and his aunts.

We used to put the olives in *'o tascappan,* a large round basket with a bag on the bottom, which we emptied into a large sack. Then the olives were placed in a pile to mature and ripen for a few days in the *granaio,* our food pantry. They were black and hard when we picked them. After a few days they became softer, which meant they were ripe, had less acidity, and were ready to bring to *'o muntan,* the oil presser. At that point we put them in burlap sacks and loaded them on the *carro,* the wagon, and brought them to *'o muntan.* Di Vincenzo Manera was the oil presser of Sant' Agata, and he was known by the old nickname carried for generations in his family as *sciucquagliello,* meaning a person with a goat lap, or someone who wore big flashy earrings. In the *frantoio,* the olive crusher, which ground up the olives, consisted of two massive motorized stone wheels that would go around and around, crushing the olives, including the pits, into a paste that had the consistency of dark mud.

After the olives were crushed, they loaded the press with layers of olive paste and soft woolen disks. Then they stacked the layers to a certain height and lowered the press, squeezing the paste and disks together and a dark green liquid would come out. The liquid then went through a pipe into the next room, to the *separatore,* which separated and removed excess liquid in the olives from the oil. After the separation, the olive oil was placed in *damigiane,* fifteen-gallon green-glass jugs. When the olive oil was fresh, it was green, and as it refined itself, the sediment settled to the bottom and the oil turned a beautiful golden color.

(left) Olive Groves in Faggiano

Spaghetti aglio e uóglio

Spaghetti Aglio e Uóglio
Spaghetti with Garlic and Oil

SERVES 4
PREPARATION TIME: 20 MINUTES

1 pound spaghetti

½ cup extra virgin olive oil

6 cloves garlic, slivered

½ cup chopped fresh Italian parsley

Salt and freshly ground black pepper

Timing is very important when making this dish. Start by heating a pot of salted water on high heat. When the water begins to boil, add the spaghetti and follow the instructions on the package for *al dente*. At this point, heat the oil in a frying pan over medium heat, add garlic, and cook until golden. Remove from the heat and add a good pinch of parsley and salt and black pepper to taste. Drain pasta when ready, reserving a little of the cooking water, and add the spaghetti to the oil. Add a few spoonfuls of pasta water to the pasta, using your judgment so as to keep it from becoming overly wet or dry. Sprinkle with more parsley and stir. Using pasta tongs, place spaghetti in bowls. Spoon any remaining oil in the pan over each dish. Sprinkle with the rest of the parsley and eat immediately. A sign of good *aglio e uóglio* is many oil spots on your shirt!

Optional: You can add anchovies, peperoncino (crushed dried hot red pepper), or both. Anchovies should be finely cut and added to the pan at the same time as the garlic. Peperoncino should be added at the same time as the salt and pepper.

Olive groves near the ancient Samnite city of Saticula

Pane i Casa Arrustut cu l'Aglio e Uóglio
Toasted Peasant Bread
with Garlic and Oil

SERVES 4

PREPARATION TIME: 10-15 MINUTES

4 slices peasant bread, approximately 1 inch thick

4 whole peeled garlic cloves

½ cup extra virgin olive oil

Toast bread on both sides until golden brown and place on a dish.

Take a clove of garlic and rub on one side of each slice of bread, using one clove for each slice. Drizzle the olive oil over each slice of bread.

When I was a little boy, my mother sometimes made this bread with sugar rather than garlic, which all the kids loved. She used to say, *"Silvio, vieni cá a bella mamma, a te, tu faccio cu zuccariell."* (Silvio, mom loves you, I'll make bread with sugar for you.)

Water fountain in the hills of Avellino with the inscription, "Bevi e Ringrazia a Dio," Drink and Thank God

Chapter 16
Home Remedies

'O meglio medico è 'u patut.
The best doctor is the one who has suffered.

In farming communities around Sant' Agata there was little medical care available, and doctor visits were often rare occasions. Families often relied on country folk medicine, using the medicinal properties of local plants and herbs to cure all kinds of ailments. A few drops of warm olive oil or a woman's breast milk were prescribed treatments for earaches. Infants were given *'o latt ra ciuccia,* donkey's milk, because its nutrients were believed to be closest to the nutrients of a mother's breast milk. Stomachaches were treated with roots of the malva plant. These were boiled for two hours to extract the minerals, and then the broth was strained through cheesecloth and drunk like a tea, with sugar. This was followed by stomach massages with warm olive oil. Children ate raw garlic and wore garlic collars to ward off influenza. Eating raw onions was thought to guard against malaria, the scourge of the South. Raw potatoes were rubbed on burns. *Brodino di pollo,* chicken soup, was often made for colds. People abided by an old aphorism based on home remedies: *stipa a mele quando ti vene a tosse*—save all your apples up for when you have a cough. More broadly, this saying also meant to always save for a rainy day.

My mother Maria often made *zuppa e fasul,* bean soup, for me in a special way that I loved. After the dish was ready, she let it sit for a few minutes so the bread soaked up all the juice. With a large fork she mashed it all up like mashed potatoes. I didn't like eating raw onions, but she made me because she used to tell stories of how onions were good medicine to fight malaria.

Ricotto di Mele Annurca
Remedy for a Cough

MAKES ABOUT 4 CUPS OF TEA

5 cups water

⅓ cup sugar

2 apples, washed and cut in quarters, unpeeled

2 large bay leaves

4 teaspoons honey, for serving

In a small pan, boil all ingredients over medium heat until the apples get soft and start to fall apart and the liquid is substantially reduced. Add 1 teaspoon of honey to each serving. Drink while good and hot. *A Salute!*

Vino Cuotto
Remedy for a Cold

We used to harvest our own honey. We had wooden boxes for the *api*, the honeybees. They used to come around in swarms looking for a place to build their honeycombs. We knew they would come sometime in July, and my uncles and my father got pots and pans to bang together and make noise. Hearing the noise attracted them to enter these boxes, where they built their honeycombs. They went out of these boxes to get nectar from the flowers. My grandfather used to put on a protective suit and a handmade glass helmet with a scarf to cover and protect his neck and long gloves, and pull out the sheets of honeycombs loaded with honey, which we used for medicinal purposes. We made *vino cuotto* and stored it for later use. We used it as a topping over ice, like a snow cone. Every once in a while, we'd get a few flakes of snow, and we'd rush out, gather it up, and bring it in the house and pour *vino cuotto* over it.

2 cups red wine, preferably homemade

¼ cup sugar

Zest of ½ lemon

Zest of ½ orange

2 sticks cinnamon

In a small pot, boil all over medium heat until the volume

is reduced by half. Drink, put on a heavy blanket and wool hat, and get right to bed. After breaking a good sweat, you can put on fresh clothes and feel better in the morning.

I Sfumient' con l'Aqua Della Escarola
Remedy for a Head Cold

This method for curing head congestion is something like a Turkish steam bath, except it's localized, just for your head.

2 heads escarole

1 large pot half full of water

1 large towel

In a pot on high heat, bring water to a boil. Add escarole and let cook for about 10 to 15 minutes. Turn heat off and hold your head over the pot. With a towel over your head that falls around the pot so that the steam doesn't escape, breathe in through your nose for approximately 10 minutes.

Remedio pu Male i Gola
Remedy for Laryngitis

Around our area in a lot of the local towns, there were professional singers who used to go to music school in Naples and they used to treat their voices with a steady diet of this remedy while they practiced singing. In our families, we also used it as a remedy for laryngitis or when our vocal chords became hoarse.

1 cup of hot tea

2 teaspoons pure honey

Slowly stir the honey into the tea and drink slowly and your throat and voice will begin to feel better

Remedio pu Male i Mole
Remedy for Toothache

This remedy for a toothache was mostly used by older people since they had more dental problems than we kids.

1 cup red wine vinegar

2 teaspoons salt

Warm up the vinegar to lukewarm temperature and stir in the salt. Take a sip and swirl it around your mouth for a moment or two. Spit it out. Repeat this until the drink is finished. After five minutes you should begin to feel better.

Remedio pu Male i Rinucchio
Remedy for a Swollen Knee

When we hurt our knees playing soccer as children, my grandmother would notice the injury and say to us, *"Vien ccà, a bella ra nonna, mo tacconcía io,"* (Come here, grandmother loves you, I'll fix it up for you). Then she'd go into her garden and pick two large fresh cabbage leaves and wrap them around the hurt knee.

2 large Savoy cabbage Leaves

1 long ace bandage

1 roll of white medical tape

Place the cabbage leaves on your knee and wrap the bandage over the cabbage, around the knee. Firm up the bandage with white medical tape to hold it in place and wear it for several hours. Repeat with fresh leaves if necessary.

Remedio pu Male i Stommaco
Remedy for an Upset Stomach

This is a two-part treatment my grandmother used when the children in the family had bad stomachaches.

1½ cups lukewarm water in a glass

1 lemon

2 teaspoons sugar

¼ cup olive oil at lukewarm temperature

Cut the lemon in half and squeeze the juice into the glass of lukewarm water, adding the 2 teaspoons of sugar. Stir and then drink slowly. Massage the belly with the olive oil.

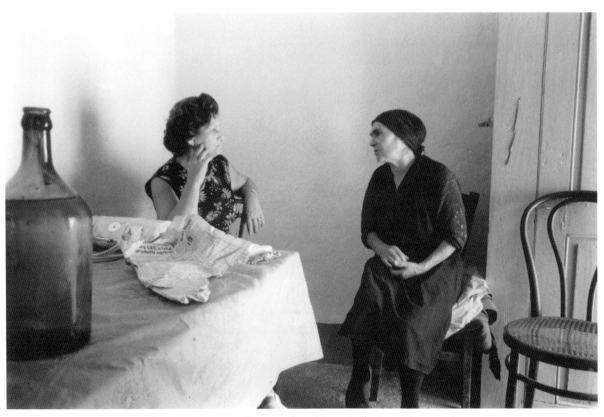

Women conversing in the town of Sippiciano, in the Aurunci Mountains

Chapter 17

Leaving for America

'U sazzio nu crer 'u riun.

The person with the full stomach doesn't believe the hungry one.

Silvio's grandfather Angelo played an important role in the story of how authentic Campanian cuisine arrived in America. In the late 1800s, *massari*, farmers who owned small parcels of land, earned the equivalent of eighty dollars a year; *braccianti*, day laborers, about fifty cents a day during planting and harvest seasons. In Naples, the typical industrial wage amounted to fifty cents for a twelve-hour day, equivalent to the cost of eight pounds of macaroni; it took four days of work to buy a pair of shoes at the market rate of two dollars a pair. Women laborers and factory workers earned even less at the daily wage of thirty cents. The *Risorgimento*'s failure to unite Italy manifested itself in the Piedmont government's worsening of already desperate economic conditions in the south by increasing taxes to fund northern school systems, industry, and infrastructure.

In 1901, fifteen-year-old Angelo Izzo joined the growing ranks of poor farmers who were leaving Italy for the United States with hopes of earning enough American dollars to realize the dream of returning home to buy farmland. Employed as a water boy on the railroad in New York, he returned to Italy to fight in World War I and later made several trips back and forth, working and saving enough American money to buy a small farm in the Contrada Sanquinito.

Daily life in Contrada Sanquinito during Silvio's boyhood in the late 1940s and early 1950s remained mired in the region's feudal past, with vast tracts of farmland owned by a few *latifondisti*, traditional wealthy landowners who had inherited the land and rented farms without capital investment and with little interest in them other than collecting profits. As late as the 1950s, there were only dirt roads and no running water. The first television arrived in 1957 and people crammed into the home of Silvio's uncle Lorenzo as though it were a theatre to watch the *Telegiornale*, the daily news. Townspeople began using small burners fueled by propane tanks rather than fireplaces to cook,

Naples, 1973

Bay of Naples, early morning

while small refrigerators replaced salting as a means of serving perishable foods. Motors replaced mules to turn wheels for grinding wheat and raising buckets from wells. Washing machines replaced the centuries-old *lavatoio*, open-arched buildings with pools of running river water where townswomen washed clothes by hand. When electric lights magically went on in homes in Sant' Agata in the mid 1950s, it was an occasion for a *festa*, the streets illuminated for the first time to the amazement of the townspeople.

Silvio grew up listening intently to his grandfather Angelo's stories about the American dream and his experiences in New York at the turn of the century. During a family wedding in town, he met sixteen-year-old Vittoria Del Monaco, a recent émigré to America whom he had played with in the streets of Contrada Sanquinito as a child. The two fell in love during her visit. Silvio faithfully followed the southern code of honor, stating his inten-tion to marry Vittoria to her mother, who would decide whether he was a good match for her young daughter. On the day before she returned to America, Vittoria's mother promised Silvio that *se vo' Dio*, if God wills it, they would someday get married. Love letters between the two were always intercepted by her mother, who made sure Silvio's intentions were noble.

On September 1, 1968, Silvio left the *contrada* to marry Vittoria and pursue his dream of becoming a master chef in America. On the night before his departure from the Bay of Naples, a large gathering of family and friends met at his home for an emotional goodbye. Amidst tearful last-minute pleas from the family to reconsider his decision to leave, grandfather Angelo took his young grandson aside, patted him on the back, and said to him softly, "*Stai contento, bello nonno, vai in America, perche è una terra santa.*" Be happy, grandfather loves you, go to America. It is a blessed land.

Silvio Suppa on a hill above the city of Sant' Agata de' Goti

Bibliography

Adamson, Melitta Weiss. *Regional Cuisines of Medieval Europe.* New York: Routledge, 2002.

Buonomo, Antonio. *Guida alla lettura della Città di Sant' Agata de' Goti.* Castelvenere: Edizioni Samnium Medica, 2008.

Campania. Milano: Italian Touring Club, 1981.

Chiarelli, Leonard, C. *Muslim Sicily (872–1072).* Malta: Midsea Books, 2010.

Caratelli, Giovanni P. *Magna Grecia.* Milano: Electra, 1988.

Corvino, Claudio. *Guida Insolita ai misteri, ai segreti, alle leggende e alle curiosità della Campania.* Roma: Newton and Compton, 2002.

Covello, Leonard. *The Social Background of the Italo-American Schoolchild.* Totowa: Rowman and Littlefield, 1972.

Di Schino, June and Furio Luccichenti. *Il Cuoco Segreto Dei Papi.* Rome: Gangemi, 2007.

Glazer, Nathan, and Daniel P. Moynihan. *Beyond the Melting Pot.* Cambridge: MIT Press, 1970.

Jenkins, Nancy H. *Cucina del Sole.* New York: HarperCollins, 2007.

Lambertino, Egano, Enrico Volpe, and Antonio Guizzaro. *Miseria e Nobiltà.* Napoli: Edizioni Scientifiche Cuzzolin, 1999.

Lantieri, Lorenzo. *Le Parole Di Origine Araba Nella Lingua Italiana.* Padua: Dottoressa Rosaria Zanetel Katrib, 1991.

Pelligrini, Fernando. *Profesione Cuoco.* Milano: Fabbri, 1968.

Rodinson, Maxime, A. J. Arberry, and Charles Perry. *Medieval Arab Cookery.* Wiltshire: Cromwell Press, 2001.

Russo, Carlo. *La Taverna Saticula.* Unpublished manuscript.

Salmon, E. T. *Samnium and the Samnites.* Cambridge: Cambridge University Press, 1967.

Salzano, Antonio. *Vocabolario Napoletano-Italiano.* Napoli: S.E.N., 1980.

Schiavelli, Vincent. *Bruculino, America.* New York: Houghton Mifflin, 1998.

Schwartz, Arthur. *Naples at Table.* New York: New York: HarperCollins, 1998.

Snowden, Frank M. *Naples in the Time of Cholera, 1884–1911.* Cambridge: Cambridge University Press, 1995.

Williams, Phyllis. *South Italian Folkways in Europe and America.* New Haven: Yale University Press, 1938.

(left) Doorway in the town of Sant' Agata de' Goti

Large farm surrounded by vineyard, dugenta, province of Benevento, Campania

Photographs

〜〜〜〜〜〜〜〜〜〜〜〜〜〜〜〜〜〜〜〜〜〜〜〜〜〜〜〜〜〜〜〜〜〜〜

Cultivating olive trees on the Amalfi coast

Index